ACCLAIM FOR DAVID MAMET's

ROMANCE

"Fitfully funny. . . . Zestful. . . . Mamet stirs a goulash of ingredients: campy jokes, rococo slurring, sexual innuendo and frivolity over Middle East peace."
— *Time Out New York*

"Mamet's funniest play ever. . . . How wickedly and well Mamet puts everything together. It's a dazzler."
— *The Star-Ledger*

"*Romance* mixes elements of W. S. Gilbert–style satire, Marx Brothersesque anarchy and, above all, Lenny Bruce–like shock tactics." — *The New York Times*

"Deliriously funny. . . . Inspired. . . . In *Romance*, Mamet is at his most adept." — *Associated Press*

DAVID MAMET

ROMANCE

David Mamet was born in Chicago in 1947. He studied at
Goddard College in Vermont and at the Neighborhood
Playhouse School of Theater in New York. He has taught
at Goddard College, the Yale School of Drama, and
New York University, and lectures at the Atlantic Theater
Company, of which he is a founding member. He is the
author of the plays *The Cryptogram*, *Oleanna*, *Speed-the-
Plow*, *Glengarry Glen Ross*, *American Buffalo*, and *Sexual
Perversity in Chicago*. He has also written screenplays for
such films as *House of Games* and the Oscar-nominated
The Verdict, as well as *The Spanish Prisoner*, *The Winslow
Boy*, and *Wag the Dog*. His plays have won the Pulitzer
Prize and the Obie Award.

ALSO BY DAVID MAMET

ROMANCE

✦ ✦ ✦

ROMANCE

✦ ✦ ✦

A Play

DAVID MAMET

VINTAGE BOOKS

A DIVISION OF RANDOM HOUSE, INC.

NEW YORK

A VINTAGE ORIGINAL, OCTOBER 2005

Library of Congress Cataloging-in-Publication Data
Mamet, David.
Romance : a play / David Mamet.
p. cm.
"A Vintage original"—T.p. verso.
1. New York (N.Y.)—Drama. I. Title.
[DNLM: 1. Legal drama. 1csh]
PS3563.A4345R66 2005
812'.54—dc22
2005048460

Vintage ISBN-10: 0-307-27518-3
Vintage ISBN-13: 978-0-307-27518-9

www.vintagebooks.com

Printed in the United States of America
10 9 8 7 6 5 4 3 2 1

ROMANCE

✦   ✦   ✦

PRODUCTION NOTES

Romance received its world premiere on March 1, 2005, at the Atlantic Theater Company, New York. Neil Pepe, Artistic Director; Andrew D. Hamingson, Managing Director.

THE PROSECUTOR	Bob Balaban
THE DEFENDANT	Steven Goldstein
THE DEFENSE ATTORNEY	Christopher Evan Welch
THE JUDGE	Larry Bryggman
THE BAILIFF	Steven Hawley
BERNARD	Keith Nobbs
THE DOCTOR	Jim Frangione

Director	Neil Pepe
Set Designer	Robert Brill
Lighting Designer	James F. Ingalls
Costume Designer	Sarah Edwards
Sound Designer	Obadiah Eaves
Casting Director	Bernard Telsey Casting
Fight Director	Rick Sordelet
Production Stage Manager	Matthew Silver
Production Manager	Kurt Gardner
General Manager	Melinda Berk

SCENE ONE

✦ ✦ ✦

A courtroom.

The JUDGE *is on the bench. The* DEFENDANT *is being interrogated by a* PROSECUTOR. *The* DEFENSE ATTORNEY *sits at the defense bench. A* BAILIFF *stands at the side.*

PROSECUTOR: Who is this . . . ?

(*All turn to sound of siren—as of motorcade passing in the streets.*)

PROSECUTOR: Who is the person in the hotel room?

DEFENDANT: I have no idea.

PROSECUTOR: You were there. You were seen there.

DEFENDANT: By whom?

PROSECUTOR: Just answer the question please.

DEFENDANT: Then, please may I be addressed with one? (*Pause*) Would you please address me with a question? (*Pause*) "You were seen there" is not a question.

PROSECUTOR: Just answer the question as you've been directed.

DEFENDANT: Well, you ask the questions, and I will attempt to answer them.

DEFENSE ATTORNEY: Your Honor, my client is endeavoring . . .

PROSECUTOR: Excuse me?

DEFENSE ATTORNEY: . . . to respond to the questions.

PROSECUTOR: Oh, *please* . . .

DEFENSE ATTORNEY: "Oh, please?" Your Honor? I must object. This scurrilous, this sad . . .

PROSECUTOR: May we be spared the . . .

DEFENSE ATTORNEY: This sense of "weariness," this false, adopted, what is it? A "charade"? A "vaudeville" . . . ?

PROSECUTOR: Your Honor, I object, I most strenuously object.

JUDGE: One moment. May we not have Peace? (*Pause*) Is that such a strange word? You will forgive me if I pontificate a moment. Will you? If I speak of Peace. Is that not the theme of the week?

PROSECUTOR: It is the theme of the weak. The theme of the strong, Your Honor, if I may, is truth.

JUDGE: Yes. Thank you. The theme of *this* week. This week's theme. Is it not peace? If not, why are they gathered here? Why are they all come here, if not for peace?

PROSECUTOR: It is a signal Honor, may it please the court. To welcome them.

(*Sound of sirens. All listen.*)

JUDGE: And there they go. And there they go. The great men. On their way to the Peace Conference . . .

(*General murmur.*)

JUDGE: Mark your calendars, people. It's a Red Letter Day. Indeed it is.

DAVID MAMET

DEFENSE ATTORNEY: Indeed it is.

JUDGE: It Honors our fair city, and it Honors us. To see those who have come so far. (*He sneezes.*)

BAILIFF: Gesundheit.

JUDGE: Thank you. And. On our way to work today. The faces. Lining the streets. Perhaps you saw them? This man or that woman. Enemies, perhaps, certainly no more than strangers. Reaching out. Because of our Visitors. Yes. Yes. We have strife. But, but, their presence here . . . (*Almost sneezes, but holds it*) I'm sorry, did I take my pill?

BAILIFF: You did, Your Honor.

JUDGE: Thank you. Instructs us, that perhaps, the aim of strife is not Victory. No, but simple peace.

ALL: Mmmm.

JUDGE: (*Pause*) I'm sorry to've taken your time. Continue. (*Pause*)

PROSECUTOR: Thank you, Your Honor . . . did you contact . . . ?

DEFENDANT: No.

8

PROSECUTOR: I must ask you to . . . refrain from interrupting.

DEFENDANT: Might I have a glass of water?

JUDGE: Get him a glass of water.

DEFENDANT: Thank you, Your Honor.

(*The* BAILIFF *brings the* DEFENDANT *a glass of water.*)

PROSECUTOR: Let me begin again. Did you physically contact a person in Room . . .

JUDGE: . . . and could someone get my pill, please . . . ?

BAILIFF: Your Honor, you've taken your pill.

JUDGE: I took my pill?

BAILIFF: Your Honor, yes.

PROSECUTOR: Do you require me to repeat the definition of "contact"?

DEFENDANT: I do not.

PROSECUTOR: I will ask you once again. Do you require me to repeat the definition?

JUDGE: I took my pill, then why do I have to sneeze?

(*The* BAILIFF *brings a vial of pills. The* JUDGE *sneezes.*)

BAILIFF: Gesundheit, Your Honor.

DEFENSE ATTORNEY: Gesundheit.

JUDGE: Thank you.

PROSECUTOR: Your Honor, I do not wish to descend to the "picayune," but as my colleague has wished you Gesundheit, I feel that I must wish you Gesundheit.

JUDGE: Thank you.

PROSECUTOR: In fairness to the State.

JUDGE: Thank you.

PROSECUTOR: Gesundheit.

JUDGE: Thank you. (*Pause*) Where were we?

PROSECUTOR: (*To the* DEFENDANT) Do you require me to repeat the definition of . . .

JUDGE: Because, I don't know about you people, but I'm moved. Yes. Yes. One becomes callous. But yes, again, we may learn. When we see Two Warring Peoples, Arabs and Jews, an Ancient Enmity. Opposed since Bible times, I'm sorry. I'm moved. Did anyone see the parade?

DEFENDANT: I did, Your Honor.

PROSECUTOR: I did, Your Honor, too.

JUDGE: I was moved, I'm sorry. (*Sneezes*)

ALL: (*Pause*) Gesundheit.

PROSECUTOR: All right. You are a chiropodist, are you not?

DEFENDANT: I am not.

PROSECUTOR: Your Honor, I ask that the defendant be instructed to . . .

DEFENDANT: I am a chiropractor.

PROSECUTOR: I beg your pardon, I intended to say chiropractor. You are a chiropractor, are you not?

DEFENDANT: I am.

JUDGE: And I would like to apologize for being late.

DEFENSE ATTORNEY: Not at all, Your Honor.

JUDGE: You people are giving up *your* time, I see no reason why I should subject you to any further, uh, uh . . .

PROSECUTOR: Not at all, Your Honor.

DEFENSE ATTORNEY: That's very gracious of you.

JUDGE: Curiously, I was late because of the parade. I took my *pill*, but I could not remember if I had taken my pill. As they do tend to make one groggy. So I returned to my house. To, to, to take my "pill"; which rendered me late as, on my *leaving* the house, I encountered the Parade. (*Pause*) I would have been on time if not for the . . . (*Pause*)

DEFENSE ATTORNEY: Of course, Your Honor.

JUDGE: Parade. A policeman. *Stopped* them, for a moment. Just to let me through. He didn't have to do that. He had no idea who I am. Call me a Weepy Old Fool. (*Pause*)

PROSECUTOR: All right. When, could you tell me, please, did you last leave the country?

DEFENDANT: Thank you, Your Honor, for the water.

JUDGE: I need a glass of water, too.

(BAILIFF *goes for the glass of water.*)

PROSECUTOR: When did you last leave the country?

JUDGE: Because I have to take my pill.

DEFENDANT: *This* country?

JUDGE: I mentioned the parade.

PROSECUTOR: Indeed, Your Honor did. (*Pause*)

JUDGE: Good.

PROSECUTOR: (*To the* DEFENDANT) Is this your signature?

DEFENDANT: (*Pause*) I do not know.

PROSECUTOR: Does it appear to be your signature? (*Pause*)

DEFENDANT: I don't know.

JUDGE: So many people. But, I suppose, that's the *nature* of a parade.

(*A slight susurrus of appreciation*)

PROSECUTOR: Surely you know if it's your signature?

DEFENDANT: I . . .

PROSECUTOR: Is it *like* your signature?

DEFENDANT: Yes.

PROSECUTOR: In what way? (*Pause*)

DEFENDANT: . . . it is written . . . it is written similarly to my signature . . .

PROSECUTOR: It *is* . . . (*Pause*)

DEFENDANT: I just said so.

PROSECUTOR: Similarly to your signature. Fine.

JUDGE: I guess what I am trying to say is this: We get caught up in the "form," the Law, Religion, Nationality . . . uh . . . skin color. And then, and then, *miraculously, miraculously*, now and then, and by the grace of God, we are free. And see, that, underneath, we love each other.

ALL: Mmm.

JUDGE: That two world leaders, steeped in *enmity* . . . (*Pause*)

PROSECUTOR: Momentous days, Your Honor.

DEFENSE ATTORNEY: Yes, momentous days, Your Honor.

JUDGE: I think we can so stipulate.

(*Laughter from the two attorneys.*)

JUDGE: And I'm not even Jewish . . .

PROSECUTOR: On the date in question . . .

JUDGE: You know, I'd like to take that back. I don't even know why I say "not even." I believe a more "neutral" expression might have been "And I'm not Jewish." (*Pause*) Proceed.

PROSECUTOR: How does this signature differ from your signature? (*Pause*)

DEFENDANT: I don't know.

PROSECUTOR: You said this resembles your signature In Part.

DEFENDANT: I did . . .

PROSECUTOR: Let me *suggest* to you that I would like you to *inform* me in what way this *differs* from your signature. (*Pause*)

DEFENDANT: I don't know.

PROSECUTOR: Then would you say they are the same?

JUDGE: One moment.

PROSECUTOR: Yes, Your Honor.

JUDGE: The pills, I believe, have made me "drowsy," and I beg your pardon, but, if you'd indulge me: What is the difference, between a chiropodist and a chiropractor?

DEFENDANT: A chiropractor aligns the spine, to create both physical and spiritual harmony.

JUDGE: And the other fellow?

DEFENDANT: He rubs people's feet.

JUDGE: For *pay*? (*Pause*)

DEFENDANT: Yes, Your Honor.

JUDGE: And you're *which*, now?

DEFENSE ATTORNEY: Your Honor, my client is a chiropractor. (*Pause*)

PROSECUTOR: All right. Do you deny this is your signature?

DEFENDANT: May I have a moment? (*He goes into conference with his attorney.*)

JUDGE: (*To* BAILIFF) Jimmy: Is it hot in here?

BAILIFF: Would Your Honor like the window opened?

DEFENDANT: I can neither deny nor affirm that signature is mine.

PROSECUTOR: What would assist you?

(*Pause. Conference between* DEFENDANT *and his* ATTORNEY)

JUDGE: No, no, I think I prefer the heat to the noise.

DEFENDANT: I cannot say that there is any *thing* which would assist me.

JUDGE: Because it's *noisy*. Well it's *noisier* because of the *parade* . . . (*Pause*) So much of life is a choice, between the lesser of two evils. (*Pause*) I suppose that's what I'm *here* for . . .

ALL: (*Dutiful laughter*)

(*Pause*)

JUDGE: They rub people's feet for "pay."

DEFENDANT: Yes. Your Honor.

JUDGE: Ah, well . . .

DEFENDANT: I quite agree, Your Honor. (*Pause*)

PROSECUTOR: I have here a document, which bears your signature. Do you recognize it?

DEFENDANT: It is a check.

PROSECUTOR: It is one of your checks. It bears your account number. Your name is printed on it. It was signed by you. Do you . . . and it was honored by the bank. Do you acknowledge it to be your signature? Let me put it differently: Do you *dispute* it?

DEFENDANT: May I have a rest?

PROSECUTOR: Do you dispute it? A check. In the amount of this credit card bill. The bill contains a charge for two airfares. Here is the credit card slip. Signed by you.

JUDGE: You know . . .

PROSECUTOR: Your Honor, if I might continue, here is the check signed by you. Both signatures were accepted as valid, one by the travel agency, one by the bank. You disputed neither.

DEFENDANT: I might have gone to Hawaii.

PROSECUTOR: Ah.

DEFENDANT: But that would not be said to be leaving the country.

PROSECUTOR: Perhaps you would confine yourself to responding to my questions.

DEFENDANT: It is not leaving the country.

PROSECUTOR: What is not?

DEFENDANT: A trip to Hawaii.

PROSECUTOR: You *went* to Hawaii?

DEFENDANT: I did not say that.

PROSECUTOR: Yes you did.

DEFENDANT: But . . . but . . . might I . . . might I finish? *Might* I finish? Might I have an opportunity to *explain* myself? Do you think? In the midst of this, this . . . in the midst of this inquisition? (*Pause*) Do you think? As one human being, speaking to another? I might *do* that?

PROSECUTOR: Might I suggest if you wish to have the proceedings terminated happily and quickly you might do well to respond to my questions? Now. Did you, in the months in question, leave the *Mainland*?

DEFENDANT: (*Pause*) I do not recall.

JUDGE: What?

PROSECUTOR: He does not recall.

JUDGE: I'm sorry. I'm sorry. My mind was drifting. He does not recall what?

PROSECUTOR: If he left the Mainland.

JUDGE: Isn't that something one would know?

PROSECUTOR: I quite agree, Your Honor.

JUDGE: Don't you know, son, if you left the Mainland?

DEFENDANT: I don't recall, sir.

PROSECUTOR: What would assist you?

DEFENDANT: I don't know.

PROSECUTOR: Let me understand you: you do not know if . . .

DEFENDANT: I don't know. Yes.

PROSECUTOR: If you left the Mainland.

JUDGE: The Mainland of what, please? (*Pause*)

PROSECUTOR: Of, of the Continent.

JUDGE: And he doesn't *know* that . . . ?

DEFENDANT: That is right. (*Pause*)

PROSECUTOR: Do you *feel*. Let me put it differently: In your *experience* in this . . . is such a recollection within the abilities of a reasonable man? (*Pause*)

DEFENDANT: I don't understand.

PROSECUTOR: . . . I withdraw the question. And I ask you at this point, if you are suggesting Mental Incapacity.

DEFENSE ATTORNEY: Your Honor . . .

PROSECUTOR: Do you suggest your inability to retain a date, or movement on your part, over the course of a year, do you put it forth as evidence of Mental Incapacity? Yes or no.

DEFENSE ATTORNEY: Your Honor, please, this is unnecessary. This is . . .

DEFENDANT: If I asked you:

PROSECUTOR: I beg your pardon, I am not the issue here.

DEFENDANT: If I asked *anyone*. (*Pause*) Some . . . some. Would have a . . . how can you say it is Mental Incapacity? That's, that's. Vicious. To offer that, excuse me, sir, that's . . . *anyone* might. Misremember, or . . .

JUDGE: That's correct . . .

PROSECUTOR: Yes?

JUDGE: Yes, in a busy life . . .

PROSECUTOR: . . . anyone might disremember . . .

DEFENDANT: Or have difficulty remembering . . .

PROSECUTOR: Yes . . .

DEFENDANT: A *date*, or . . . that, that . . . that is, just . . .

PROSECUTOR: You're saying that's Human Nature.

DEFENDANT: Absolutely.

JUDGE: That is Human Nature. Fellas. Just this morning, I, uh . . . (*Pause*) People Forget.

PROSECUTOR: You've said that you have difficulty with your memory. That's right. It is Human Nature. Yes. It is. How does one deal with it?

JUDGE: Is it hot in here? (*Lays his head down on the desk.*)

DEFENDANT: One, one has, they have Agendas, or . . .

PROSECUTOR: People have difficulty remembering, so they have Agendas.

DEFENDANT: Yes.

PROSECUTOR: Which they would trust more than their recollections.

DEFENDANT: Yes. That is the purpose of them.

PROSECUTOR: That they would prefer notations on a scrap of paper.

DEFENDANT: As you know.

JUDGE: (*Lifts his head up*) If we could move it along, gentlemen, I am not feeling too . . .

PROSECUTOR: . . . if it please the court.

JUDGE: I find I'm not feeling too well.

PROSECUTOR: With the Court's Pardon, if I might, the one instant . . .

JUDGE: I found that my mind was drifting. That's not like me.

DEFENDANT: Many times, Your Honor, sitting for long periods stresses the spine and induces a decrease in the fluid of the dural matter which may cause lapses in attention.

JUDGE: Yes, you bet, but, in truth? I thought I'd step down, just . . . just . . . (*He sneezes.*)

BAILIFF: Gesundheit, Your Honor . . .

JUDGE: Thank you. To be a part of the parade. Do you know, just to be a part of it. I wonder if the pollen in the elm trees near the consulate exacerbated my attack.

DEFENDANT: Is it elm to which Your Honor is allergic?

JUDGE: Do they have "pollen"? I suppose they'd have to, as they're "trees." They're "trees," right, Jimmy? They're "trees"? Right, *elm trees*."

BAILIFF: Your Honor?

JUDGE: Well, they say tomatoes are a fruit.

PROSECUTOR: Might we, with respect to the court, confine and limit our attention to the . . .

JUDGE: Quite quite right. I beg your pardon.

PROSECUTOR: I will be brief.

JUDGE: It stuck in my mind, because I have an allergy to Pollen.

PROSECUTOR: I . . .

JUDGE: I'm not feeling well, and, in fact, I think I'd like to call a recess.

PROSECUTOR: One moment, Your Honor, please, is all I ask.

JUDGE: *Is* there, um, pollen, in the elm?

PROSECUTOR: I don't know, Your Honor.

JUDGE: Or is that just a thing we associate with "bees." (*Pause*)

PROSECUTOR: (*To* DEFENDANT) I ask you to turn your attention to this document, and to identify it for me, please. (*Pause*) Would you identify it for me, please? Is this your agenda? For the year in question?

DEFENDANT: Yes.

PROSECUTOR: It is your name.

DEFENDANT: Yes.

PROSECUTOR: Is this your *handwriting*? (*Pause*)

DEFENDANT: I . . .

PROSECUTOR: Who is the person in the hotel?

DEFENDANT: I . . .

PROSECUTOR: Is it "B"?

DEFENDANT: I didn't . . .

PROSECUTOR: Is that a man's name?

DEFENDANT: I . . .

PROSECUTOR: "B." Does that stand for the name of a *man*?

DEFENDANT: . . . I . . .

PROSECUTOR: Is this your handwriting? Here. Would you look here, please? Here. Would you read that sign, please? (*Pause*) Would you read it please?

DEFENDANT: It appears to . . .

PROSECUTOR: What is your problem? Would you read the sign?

DEFENDANT: It appears to . . . (*Pause*)

PROSECUTOR: What is the sign?

DEFENDANT: I cannot . . .

PROSECUTOR: Is it the letter "B"?

DEFENDANT: It appears to, I . . .

PROSECUTOR: What *follows* it? (*Pause*)

DEFENDANT: It is a symbol.

PROSECUTOR: And what is the symbol? (*Pause*)

DEFENDANT: An arrow.

PROSECUTOR: An arrow. What is it pointing to?

DEFENDANT: It app . . .

PROSECUTOR: Don't tell me what it appears to be. What is it? Is it not the letter "H"? And are you going to tell me that it is a "ladder" or a "football goal"? It is the letter "H." The phrase or ideogram: "B." Arrow H, or perhaps, Hawaii . . .

DEFENSE ATTORNEY: Objection.

PROSECUTOR: . . . or: "B," to Hawaii. Is that correct?

DEFENSE ATTORNEY: Objection.

DEFENDANT: That is your understanding.

PROSECUTOR: Indeed it is.

(JUDGE *sneezes.*)

DEFENSE ATTORNEY: Gesun . . .

PROSECUTOR: One moment . . . Indeed it is, and the symbol following?

DEFENDANT: I . . .

PROSECUTOR: A "love heart"? And: following that?

DEFENSE ATTORNEY: . . . Your Honor . . .

PROSECUTOR: Is it a rabbit?

DEFENDANT: I . . .

PROSECUTOR: Is it a rabbit in quotes? Sir . . .

(JUDGE *begins sneezing again.*)

PROSECUTOR: . . . with A Happy Face? What is the happy rabbit a symbol of?

DEFENDANT: I, um, Your Honor . . . ?

DEFENSE ATTORNEY: Your Honor, if I might suggest . . . (*As the* JUDGE *continues sneezing*)

DEFENDANT: I don't think it's a rabbit . . . Your Honor, I . . .

JUDGE: Did I take my pill?

PROSECUTOR: ARE YOU GOING TO SIT THERE AND TELL ME THAT IS NOT A RABBIT . . . ? YOU LYING, SICK, PERJURED . . .

DEFENSE ATTORNEY: Objection . . .

JUDGE: (*Sneezing*) Gentlemen, gentlemen, may we not have peace?

DEFENDANT: I, I, I . . .

PROSECUTOR: Are you going to tell me that is not a *rabbit*?

DEFENSE ATTORNEY: Objection, objection, objection.

JUDGE: May we not have Peace?

DEFENDANT: I, I, I . . .

PROSECUTOR: Are you going to tell me that is not a *Rabbit* . . . ?

DEFENSE ATTORNEY: It doesn't look like a rabbit to me.

PROSECUTOR: Not everyone has the equal capacity to draw a rabbit.

DEFENSE ATTORNEY: (*Of the drawing*) What are those?

PROSECUTOR: Ears. Those are Ears, those are its Ears, They're Rabbit Ears.

DEFENSE ATTORNEY: No one could draw a rabbit that inexpertly, Your Honor . . . ?

JUDGE: Achoo.

DEFENSE ATTORNEY: No one, no one . . .

PROSECUTOR: Not everyone, Your Honor, has the God-given ability to draw a rabbit.

JUDGE: Achoo.

PROSECUTOR: I can and will present a cavalcade of Expert Witnesses . . .

JUDGE: I don't think my prescription is working . . .

PROSECUTOR: Your Honor, one moment.

JUDGE: ACHOO ACHOO ACHOO.

PROSECUTOR: Expert witnesses, who Cannot Draw a Rabbit.

JUDGE: Ah, shit, I think I'm going to have to Lay Down.

End of Scene One.

SCENE TWO

✦   ✦   ✦

Small conference room. The DEFENDANT *and the* DEFENSE
ATTORNEY. *Pause.*

DEFENSE ATTORNEY: Well, you know, it looked like a
fucken rabbit to *me*. I asked you. Didn't I ask you?
Not To Get Up On The Stand? Did I ask you that?

DEFENDANT: I . . .

DEFENSE ATTORNEY: It looked like a fucken rabbit to Me.

DEFENDANT: What if I was not there?

DEFENSE ATTORNEY: Ah hell, where?

DEFENDANT: In Hawaii.

DEFENSE ATTORNEY: I don't know anymore.

DEFENDANT: Well, I'm paying you to know. So just . . .

DEFENSE ATTORNEY: You're paying me to give you my advice. And my advice was not to get up on the stand, you *got* up . . .

DEFENDANT: Yes, I got up on the stand . . .

DEFENSE ATTORNEY: You got up there, and made a fool, not only of yourself, but . . .

DEFENDANT: I got up on the stand, because, because I feel . . .

DEFENSE ATTORNEY: And then he asked you about the Rabbit. "What were you doing in Hawaii with a Happy Rabbit?"

DEFENDANT: What if I was not there?

DEFENSE ATTORNEY: Were you there?

DEFENDANT: Would you follow me please?

DEFENSE ATTORNEY: If you were not there. One would be hard-pressed to account for the Rabbit and all. "B," Arrow, Love Heart, to Hawaii, Rabbit. If you were not there. Anyone "reading" them. Would ask you. If you were not there, would ask for your "story."

DEFENDANT: For My Story.

DEFENSE ATTORNEY: Yes.

DEFENDANT: But. (*Pause*) But would you . . . yes, I know, I understand . . . But. As an "exercise."

DEFENSE ATTORNEY: . . . we have so little . . .

DEFENDANT: Please. As a, as, as a *hypothetical Instance.* Please. In which, all right. All right? (*Pause*)

DEFENSE ATTORNEY: All right.

DEFENDANT: In which the facts seemed to be. *Seemed* to be . . .

DEFENSE ATTORNEY: Do you know, and now, he calls a *recess*. And I'm never going to be able to get home . . .

DEFENDANT: I . . .

DEFENSE ATTORNEY: . . . with the parade.

DEFENDANT: The point.

DEFENSE ATTORNEY: The point. The point is not . . .

DEFENDANT: . . . please . . .

DEFENSE ATTORNEY: May I finish: the point is not what you ad . . .

DEFENDANT: . . . I understand.

DEFENSE ATTORNEY: What you *admit*.

DEFENDANT: I understand that.

DEFENSE ATTORNEY: But . . .

DEFENDANT: . . . I underst . . .

DEFENSE ATTORNEY: But, please let me, what a reasonable person must infer from the facts.

DEFENDANT: I understand that.

DEFENSE ATTORNEY: . . . if you understand, then I am baffled by . . .

DEFENDANT: I'm asking, as a hypothetical instance.

DEFENSE ATTORNEY: I, I, I, I feel that I am being remiss in my duties.

DEFENDANT: A hypothetical instance where . . .

DEFENSE ATTORNEY: We have so little time.

DEFENDANT: If: if we postulate.

DEFENSE ATTORNEY: To indulge in: Listen to me:

DEFENDANT: I . . .

DEFENSE ATTORNEY: To indulge in. Please, all right, I know, believe me, No, I *realize* that, to you, much of the proceedings must seem, they must seem to you *arbitrary*, and . . .

(BAILIFF *enters with a newspaper.*)

BAILIFF: You fellas want lunch?

DEFENDANT: If we posit a hypothetical instance where . . .

DEFENSE ATTORNEY: You were in Hawaii. November Tenth, of last year. B arrow, love heart, Hawaii, Laughing Rabbit. You were there. How in the *fuck* are you not going to have been there?

DEFENDANT: By providing an alternative.

DEFENSE ATTORNEY: To where you were?

DEFENDANT: To, to a way of "looking" at it.

DEFENSE ATTORNEY: All right, then, after the Mumbo Jumbo, what is the alternative?

DEFENDANT: My understanding is, at that point, that is *your* job.

DEFENSE ATTORNEY: And my job is?

DEFENDANT: To, to frame an alternative . . . to present to the Judge . . .

DEFENSE ATTORNEY: A *Lie* . . . ? (*Pause*) *A LIE?*

BAILIFF: Anybody want to see the paper?

DEFENDANT: Oh, Lord, Oh Lord, now I *am* in trouble . . . now I am, truly, truly fucked. Oh, God, oh, God . . . You don't want to *lie*?

DEFENSE ATTORNEY: If you would let me do my job . . .

DEFENDANT: *Why did you* go to *Law* School? If you don't want to *Lie*?

DEFENSE ATTORNEY: (*Pause*) I . . .

BAILIFF: (*Looking at the paper*) Big doings at the peace conference . . .

DEFENDANT: You're fired. (*Pause*)

DEFENSE ATTORNEY: I fear you don't understand.

DEFENDANT: You're fff . . .

DEFENSE ATTORNEY: Can you suppose that another representation would be more to your taste?

DEFENDANT: I don't know.

DEFENSE ATTORNEY: Well, I *do* know. YOU'RE *GUILTY*. DO YOU UNDERSTAND?

DEFENDANT: I AM NOT GUILTY UNTIL A DULY CONSTITUTED COURT . . .

DEFENSE ATTORNEY: What BULLSHIT. WHAT UTTER CRAP. YOU MAKE ME SICK. YOU MAKE ME ASHAMED. I'M FILLED WITH CONTEMPT, WITH, *FUCK* CONTEMPT, WITH LOATH-ING, AND YOU SIT UP THERE, GUILTY AS SIN, CRIMINAL, SICK, PERVERTED, AND I'M . . .

DEFENDANT: . . . wait one moment . . .

DEFENSE ATTORNEY: Trying, trying, somehow to . . .

DEFENDANT: I'm paying you . . .

DEFENSE ATTORNEY: . . . a *pittance*, For what I go through? Forced to sit *next* to you, you SICK FUCK, day-after-day, *supporting* you; nodding at your infantile hypocrisies. This sick Talmudic, Jewish . . . (*Pause*) Ohmigod.

DEFENDANT: Aha.

DEFENSE ATTORNEY: I . . . I . . . I must, *most* humbly, *Most* humbly. *Beg*. Your forgiveness. My speech has run away with me, I . . . I was to take my son, my son Tommy. To the Church Youth Hockey game today, and it is. A *particularly* anxious time. As, as I am divorced, I see him seldom. And these outings, and the time we spend together. Are *precious* to us, and I am somewhat distraught. At the *probability* that I will be late, and, and I can but most sincerely Beg Your Pardon. (*Pause*)

DEFENDANT: I accept your apology.

DEFENSE ATTORNEY: Thank you. That is gracious and generous of you.

DEFENDANT: I understand your anxiety.

DEFENSE ATTORNEY: Thank you.

DEFENDANT: I know that you are a religious man . . .

DEFENSE ATTORNEY: . . . yes, I am . . .

DEFENDANT: . . . that you're taking your son to a Church Function . . .

DEFENSE ATTORNEY: . . . the Youth Hockey game . . .

DEFENDANT: . . . and that if you arrived late . . .

DEFENSE ATTORNEY: . . . yes . . .

DEFENDANT: . . . you might have trouble, getting the Priest's dick out of your son's ass.

DEFENSE ATTORNEY: You fucken kike, you sick, *sick* . . .

DEFENDANT: . . . fuck you.

DEFENSE ATTORNEY: Christkilling Jew, Cocksucking *bastard* . . .

BAILIFF: . . . you fellas want lunch?

DEFENSE ATTORNEY: (*To* BAILIFF) Fuck you, too. Fuck you, too. Fuck the Lot of you.

BAILIFF: . . . uh . . .

DEFENSE ATTORNEY: I'm done, I'm gone, I've been nixed.

DEFENDANT: You *are* fired. I say you're fired, and you walk out on me . . .

DEFENSE ATTORNEY: Fuck you . . .

DEFENDANT: Oh, oh, who's weak, now?

DEFENSE ATTORNEY: Fuck you. Call me a *liar* . . .

DEFENDANT: Is it upset, that I used One Little Word?

DEFENSE ATTORNEY: You fucking kike.

DEFENDANT: Oh, Bad Man's called him a Hypocrite . . .

DEFENSE ATTORNEY: You you you you you you you're the fucken hypocrite . . .

DEFENDANT: *Am* I . . . ?

DEFENSE ATTORNEY: You're fucken "well-told right you are, who who who, and who has to suffer for you?" (*Pause*) Uh?

DEFENDANT: Oh? *You?*

BAILIFF: (*Looking at paper and holding a pencil*) . . . prehistoric fish . . .

DEFENDANT: Oh—who suffers for my sins . . . ! "Who gave his Only Begotten Son . . ."? (*Pause*)

DEFENSE ATTORNEY: What is that supp . . .

BAILIFF: . . . prehistoric fish . . . ten letters . . .

DEFENDANT: You know what that means.

DEFENSE ATTORNEY: No. I'm not sure that I do.

DEFENDANT: No.

DEFENSE ATTORNEY: No. I'm not at all sure that I do.

DEFENDANT: Fuck you.

BAILIFF: Prehistoric fish. Ten letters.

DEFENSE ATTORNEY: Is, that, do I take that to mean . . . ?

DEFENDANT: Fuck you.

DEFENSE ATTORNEY: Fuck me? Fuck *you*, you Rug Merchant, Greasy, Hooknosed, *no*-dick, Christkilling, son-of-a-bitch sacrilegious . . .

BAILIFF: The judge says . . .

DEFENSE ATTORNEY: Fuck the Judge, and fuck *you*, and, and *you*, you mocky, sheeny *cock*sucker . . . when I've missed taking Little Tommy to Church Youth Hockey, because I'm stuck in here listening to your sniveling, sick . . .

DEFENDANT: Oh, Oh, Little Tommy, again? Limping, when he comes home from communion, does he . . . ? (*Pause*)

DEFENSE ATTORNEY: I hope, I hope that the Arabs. Rise in their droves, and drive your people into the sea. Killing the children. Raping their wives and burning down all traces of your two-thousand-year-long sacrilege.

DEFENDANT: Fuck you.

BAILIFF: . . . you having lunch . . . ?

DEFENSE ATTORNEY: And, if there *is* a God. And there is, who died for us, who suffered for Mankind, who lives today, and hears all, I pray to that God to hear my plea . . .

BAILIFF: They're having meat loaf today . . .

DEFENSE ATTORNEY: . . . that you, your family, your race . . .

BAILIFF: . . . on the steam table . . .

DEFENSE ATTORNEY: . . . I heard you. And that every sperm, seed, trace, artifact . . .

DEFENDANT: If you would be ONE BILLIONTH as persuasive Out There . . .

DEFENSE ATTORNEY: Fuck you. I'm fired, and you're screwed. Because you're going to prison. Prison. Do you hear? Because the man who (and I am that man) who stood the *remotest* chance of saving your worthless Jew self, the one man . . .

DEFENDANT: . . . if you had a fucking clue . . .

DEFENSE ATTORNEY: I don't need a clue. I don't NEED a clue. I *needed* you to stay off the stand, to . . .

DEFENDANT: Submit . . .

DEFENSE ATTORNEY: Yes. Submit. At the dentist, do you say, "They're my teeth: Let me help"? YOU NEED TO SUBMIT.

DEFENDANT: SUBMIT . . . SUBMIT SUBMIT SUB-MIT SUBMIT SUBMIT. God forgive me, what have I done? I hired a Goy lawyer! It's like going to a straight hairdresser. And now he wants me to SUBMIT. You fucken brain-dead, white socks, country club, plaid pants, Campbell's soup fucken *sheigetz* Goy. Submit. That's fine. Take the example of Your Lord.

DEFENSE ATTORNEY: . . . there I must insist you stop . . .

DEFENDANT: Your fairy tale . . . oooh, they rolled the stone away from the cave . . .

DEFENSE ATTORNEY: . . . I've warned you . . .

DEFENDANT: While the porridge cooled . . .

DEFENSE ATTORNEY: I'm not warning you again . . .

DEFENDANT: Oh. What will you do? Hitch up your pants and kill every Jew in Europe?

DEFENSE ATTORNEY: . . . it's what you deserve . . .

DEFENDANT: Hitch up your leather pants and gas everybody?

DEFENSE ATTORNEY: . . . a pogrom . . .

DEFENDANT: My very presence here. MY VERY PRESENCE HERE IS A POGROM . . .

DEFENSE ATTORNEY: . . . there it is . . .

DEFENDANT: A pogrom . . .

DEFENSE ATTORNEY: . . . you people can't order a cheese sandwich . . .

DEFENDANT: Fuck you.

DEFENSE ATTORNEY: . . . without mentioning the Holocaust.

DEFENDANT: My people do not *eat* cheese sandwiches.

DEFENSE ATTORNEY: Oh. Oh, what? It isn't "kosher" . . . ?

DEFENDANT: IT ISN'T *TASTY. TASTY.* You mindless Nazi Fuck. IT DOESN'T *TASTE* GOOD, AND SO WE DON'T *EAT* IT.

DEFENSE ATTORNEY: IS THAT SO?

DEFENDANT: Yes. Yes. We eat Christian *Children*. We bake them in *pies*, just like you have been saying these two thousand years. Your whole dolt, Catholic . . .

DEFENSE ATTORNEY: . . . I'm Episcopalian . . .

DEFENDANT: And what the fuck is *that*? A Catholic with a Volvo . . .

DEFENSE ATTORNEY: Oh, that's charming.

DEFENDANT: Go back to the Country Club. Drink, fuck each other's wives, and increase the defense budget. Fuck you.

DEFENSE ATTORNEY: . . . what's wrong with the defense budget? (*Pause*)

DEFENDANT: What's *wrong* . . . ? What's wrong with the *defense* budget? Are you *serious*?

BAILIFF: You want lunch?

DEFENSE ATTORNEY: What's *wrong*? Yes—with the Defense Budget, which, among other things, keeps the Israelis and the, the, the, Duly-Constituted Palestinian . . .

DEFENDANT: I'll *give* you the Palestinians . . . I'll . . .

DEFENSE ATTORNEY: Oh. What are they? "Hanky-Heads"?

DEFENDANT: . . . no . . .

DEFENSE ATTORNEY: Savages, who don't deserve . . .

DEFENDANT: No.

DEFENSE ATTORNEY: "Sand-Negroes" . . . ?

BAILIFF: You fellas want lunch?

DEFENSE ATTORNEY: I don't want lunch.

BAILIFF: You might want to eat. Going to be a long afternoon.

DEFENSE ATTORNEY: I'm not hungry.

BAILIFF: I was you, I'd eat. What do you eat?

DEFENDANT: What do you mean?

BAILIFF: I mean "what do you eat?"

DEFENDANT: I eat "food." What do you mean?

DEFENSE ATTORNEY: He meant, is there anything you don't eat?

DEFENDANT: There's lots of things that I eat. If they're food I eat them. Why do you ask?

DEFENSE ATTORNEY: He asked out of politeness, because you're Jewish.

DEFENDANT: How would he know that?

DEFENSE ATTORNEY: You've been shouting "goy cock-sucker" for an hour. What did he think it was? "Self-loathing"?

BAILIFF: You fellas see the parade?

DEFENSE ATTORNEY: . . . shouting like some *rug* bazaar . . .

DEFENDANT: . . . what does that mean?

DEFENSE ATTORNEY: A rug bazaar.

DEFENDANT: What does that mean, I know what you said, what does it mean?

DEFENSE ATTORNEY: It means, it means, my friend . . .

DEFENDANT: Don't start in with that.

DEFENSE ATTORNEY: With what?

DEFENDANT: With the Jew thing: "my friend." You Goy Flunky. Yes, I come from a Rug Bazaar. Yes. I'm a kike; yes, I'm a sheeny Jew. I come from the Casbah. I come from the Middle East. Two thousand years ago, when we killed your Lord. That's me. A hook-nosed greasy Jew, who would prefer the good, clean logic of a Rug . . .

DEFENSE ATTORNEY: . . . if . . .

DEFENDANT: Shut up . . . of a Rug Bazaar . . . where each has something . . . to . . .

DEFENSE ATTORNEY: If . . .

DEFENDANT: You fucken brain-dead, child molester thief *goy* monsters, and you tell me Justice? You know what true Justice is?

DEFENSE ATTORNEY: No, please tell me.

DEFENDANT: It is the Rug Bazaar.

DEFENSE ATTORNEY: Ah ha . . .

DEFENDANT: You want to solve the evils of the world? You want to know how? By reducing the discussion, to a Simple Human Need. Instead of screaming at Me, Standing Me Up in front of the Prosecutor of Judea . . . and, by the way, he was Jewish . . .

DEFENSE ATTORNEY: Who?

DEFENDANT: Christ.

DEFENSE ATTORNEY: Christ Jesus? Yes. He was a Jew. Yes. I affirm that.

DEFENDANT: Sporting of you.

DEFENSE ATTORNEY: No, I'm sick of it. I'm sick of listening to you malign my faith.

DEFENDANT: Fuck you.

DEFENSE ATTORNEY: From a chiropractor? From a "chiropractor" . . . ?

DEFENDANT: My profession, sir . . .

DEFENSE ATTORNEY: And now I've missed the hockey game . . .

DEFENDANT: My profession, sir . . .

DEFENSE ATTORNEY: . . . fuck your profession . . .

DEFENDANT: . . . was alleviating suffering when doctors dwelt in caves.

DEFENSE ATTORNEY: Through rubbing people's feet . . .

DEFENDANT: No, actually, through realignment, of the *spine* . . .

DEFENSE ATTORNEY: Oh, bullshit.

DEFENDANT: . . . realignment of the spine, excuse me, yes, which, even in the most obstinate cases . . .

DEFENSE ATTORNEY: Oh, *please* . . .

DEFENDANT: . . . brings about reversal of disease, well-*being*, right *thinking*, mental equilibrium, and . . . ohmigod . . .

DEFENSE ATTORNEY: What?

DEFENDANT: OHMIGOD.

DEFENSE ATTORNEY: *What?*

DEFENDANT: *I KNOW HOW TO BRING PEACE TO THE MIDDLE EAST!!*

End of Scene Two.

SCENE THREE

✦ ✦ ✦

The PROSECUTOR *is giving a speech to what appears to be an empty room.*

PROSECUTOR: In every time, this one or that, has introduced a New Thing. Never Before Seen Upon The Earth. And called it Bohemia. Radicalism. Freedom, this doctrine, of license, this notion that we are above the law. Based upon what? This brave announcement? The individual's sentiment of being Chosen. Laws, my friend, and laws, my neighbors, however, came into being as we learned, at long, hard cost, and both to our chagrin and to our education, that we cannot *trust* our senses. (*Pause*) See us, then calling crime "freedom." And by any other name than that set down in Law. But the Law will find you. That which first was a reminder comes again as a demand—a correction. For I, for you, no less than that man tempted, fallen, and now brought before you answers to the Law. And you who judge him must be still, and ask of yourselves honest and hard dedication. To that ideal, which *alone* can guide us— and it is a tree of life. To those who hold fast to it. (*Pause*) What do you think? (*Pause*) Tell me truly. (*Pause*) Go on. (*Pause*)

(BERNARD, *a young fellow, clad, perhaps, but in a leopard-skin posing strap, rises from the couch, where he has been hidden.*)

BERNARD: I don't know.

PROSECUTOR: . . . *Oh God.*

BERNARD: I just. I don't know.

PROSECUTOR: Oh God.

BERNARD: I . . .

PROSECUTOR: Spare me. *Spare*—

BERNARD: I . . .

PROSECUTOR: Please. Please. *Spare* me your pity.

BERNARD: It may, will you wait a second . . . it may be, it's *possible* that . . .

PROSECUTOR: . . . please . . .

BERNARD: . . . will you let me finish? It's *possible* that it's just a bit too strong.

PROSECUTOR: What in the *world* can that mean? (*Pause*)

BERNARD: I . . .

PROSECUTOR: What can you mean to tell me, that it is "TOO STRONG"?

BERNARD: For *me*. Too strong for *me*.

PROSECUTOR: Too strong for *you*.

BERNARD: At this *point*.

PROSECUTOR: . . . how can it be Too Strong?

BERNARD: I . . .

PROSECUTOR: Could I, do you think, would you just, for God's sake, say that you don't *like* it?

BERNARD: No, that's not the case.

PROSECUTOR: It *is* the case. (*Pause*)

BERNARD: I . . .

PROSECUTOR: (*Simultaneous with above*) Do you have any notion how *humiliating* this is . . . ? (*Pause*)

BERNARD: I . . .

PROSECUTOR: (*Simultaneous with above*) . . . to indulge in this *hypocrisy*.

BERNARD: I . . . (*Pause*)

PROSECUTOR: Well, fine, fine. What would you change?

BERNARD: I . . .

PROSECUTOR: What?

BERNARD: I *do* like it.

PROSECUTOR: That was not my question.

BERNARD: I . . .

PROSECUTOR: Would you, would you please, for the love of God? Please. (*Pause*) Would you *please?* (*Pause*) For God's sake? (*Pause*) You follow me . . . ?

BERNARD: I . . .

PROSECUTOR: Would you just leave me alone for a while? (*Pause*) Do you think?

BERNARD: I'm sorry if I hurt you.

PROSECUTOR: I'm sure that you are. (*Pause*) I know that you are.

BERNARD: I . . .

PROSECUTOR: . . . seriously. (*Pause*)

BERNARD: Thank you. (*Pause*)

PROSECUTOR: If I could just be *alone* for a while. (BERNARD *starts to speak*.) Yes. No. I know. (*Pause*) *Thank* you. (*Pause*) Thank you. I mean that seriously. I just want to be alone.

BERNARD: I don't want you to be angry with me.

PROSECUTOR: I'm not angry with you.

BERNARD: I'm so sorry.

PROSECUTOR: I'm not angry.

BERNARD: I . . .

PROSECUTOR: It's all right. I'm, I'm, I'm a little up . . .

BERNARD: No. Truly. I . . . I humbly beg your . . .

PROSECUTOR: WOULD YOU GET THE FUCK OUT OF HERE AND LEAVE ME ALONE? HAVE YOU ANY IDEA HOW HUMILIATING THIS IS . . .

BERNARD: I . . .

PROSECUTOR: Bullshit. *Bullshit.*

(*A smoke alarm sounds from offstage. Pause.*)

BERNARD: I . . .

PROSECUTOR: *Bullshit.* It's about *you.* It's all about *you.* How *contrite* you are. How little you demand, how . . . (*Alarm beeps twice.*)

BERNARD: . . . you . . .

PROSECUTOR: *No. Don't* say that.

BERNARD: . . . you don't . . .

PROSECUTOR: Yes. I do. This is, no. This is *not* "one of those things." And I won't have it. Do you hear? What? Have I "hurt your *feelings*"?

BERNARD: . . . I . . . (*Alarm sounds again.*)

PROSECUTOR: I'm losing you. I'm losing you. I know it. Don't lie to me. Please please please, just tell me the truth. For once, as if I were man enough to hear it. (*Alarm*)

BERNARD: You are man enough to hear it.

PROSECUTOR: I am?

BERNARD: Yes. (*Alarm*)

PROSECUTOR: To hear it.

BERNARD: Yes.

(*Alarm beeps continuously. Smoke billows in.*)

PROSECUTOR: (*Spoken over alarm*) To hear what? (*Pause*) What are we talking about? Oh, my God, now I am lost. What are we talking about? My whole world is a mass of pain. The ground is shifting under my feet, and I know, for the first time, I know what they mean. When they say, uh . . . uh . . . (*Pause*) Uh . . . what the fuck is that?

(*Phone rings as* PROSECUTOR *storms off.* BERNARD *answers the phone.*)

BERNARD: (*On phone*) Hello? He's in the kitchen. (*Pause*) Because the roast is burning is why. Because I forgot to turn it down. (*Pause*) Because I'm a dunce, all right? (*Pause*) Well, I was born that way. I suppose it's genetic. (*Pause*) A lot of people say that. (*Beeping ends.* PROSECUTOR *reenters holding the offending smoke detector*.) There's a phone call for you.

PROSECUTOR: Fuck you.

BERNARD: Fuck you, too.

PROSECUTOR: And fuck you, *too.*

BERNARD: And fuck *you.*

PROSECUTOR: (*To phone*) Hello. No. It's a fine time. It's swell. What do you want? I can't talk to you. Tell it to me tomorrow. Well, what is it you're going to *tell* me tomorrow? (*Pause*) To Suspend the prosecution? Why?

BERNARD: The roast is burnt.

PROSECUTOR: Fuck you. (*Pause. To phone*) TO DROP THE CHARGES? YOUR GUY IS AS GUILTY AS THE LORD KNOWS HOW TO MAKE HIM. (*Pause*) I don't *want* to give him a cont . . . I don't *want* to give him a continuance. Why should I give him a continuance? (*Pause*) TO TAKE PART IN THE PEACE PROCESS?

BERNARD: Tell him to go with God.

PROSECUTOR: Fuck you.

BERNARD: Fuck you, too.

PROSECUTOR: And fuck you, *too*. You little two-bit piece of fucking INTELLECTUAL FLUFF.

BERNARD: Oh, oh, oh, did you marry me for my *mind*?

PROSECUTOR: Fuck you.

BERNARD: So that we could discuss *Proust*? Was that what had you GLUED TO THE SMALL LEATHER-GOODS COUNTER AT SAKS, DAY AFTER DAY???

PROSECUTOR: Fuck you.

BERNARD: *Mooning* . . . ?

PROSECUTOR: (*To phone*) He's going to bring peace *how* . . . ?

BERNARD: I'm like, "hey, buy a *wallet* . . ."

PROSECUTOR: Fuck you.

BERNARD: You cheap *fuck*. Where do you buy your clothes? *The garbage?* "Oh, I love you, Bunny."

PROSECUTOR: Fuck you.

BERNARD: "Please, please, I know I'm fat. I know I have the taste of a Midwestern fucking pet-shop owner . . . I know I'm unworthy of you . . ."

PROSECUTOR: . . . go on.

BERNARD: "I know I have the contours of a *pear*, and I'm ashamed of myself and I'm no good in *bed*."

PROSECUTOR: Ah ha . . .

BERNARD: "And you're the loveliest thing that I've ever *seen*, and I'm unfit to even Gaze upon you," night after night. "You're like a fine beer." AND MY FRIENDS LOOKED AT YOU LIKE I'D BROUGHT HOME SOME TV *WEATHER-MAN*. But, no no no, "I love you, Bernard. And I'll make a *home* for you, and I'll *protect* you . . ."

PROSECUTOR: Are you crying? (*Pause*) Oh, are you crying?

BERNARD: Oh, do you think that's some Cheap Girlish Trick?

PROSECUTOR: (*To phone*) One moment . . .

BERNARD: Do you think that's "unfair"? To have "feelings"? "Feelings"? . . . now I've lost my contact. (BERNARD *starts crawling around on the floor.*)

PROSECUTOR: . . . go on . . .

BERNARD: . . . I've lost my contact . . .

PROSECUTOR: . . . go on . . .

BERNARD: I don't want to go on. I want to be left alone.

PROSECUTOR: Bunny . . .

BERNARD: Leave me alone.

PROSECUTOR: Bunny, I'm over here.

BERNARD: I don't care where you are. Go back to your work. Go to your priceless phone call. Go, go on with your "if it please the court," sick Macho *bullshit*: Mumbo Jumbo, Habeas Gumbo . . . I've lost my contact . . . Put the World in Prison. Maybe that will compensate you for your lack of self-esteem. I'm done. I'm done . . . I've burned the roast. *You* clean the fucking pan. I'm sorry for you. (*He exits.*)

PROSECUTOR: (*To phone*) Hello? (*Pause*) A friend. What business is it of yours? (*Pause*) Yeah, I heard you. (*Pause*) And how would that bring peace to the Middle East? (*Pause*) Well, too bad, 'cause you get your ass and your client's ass into court tomorrow at ten A.M. (*Pause*) The judge is not sick, he has hay fever. He'll be there and *you* be there . . . I don't give a fuck about the Middle East. Fuck *you*.

BERNARD: (*Reentering*) Just two things: One,

PROSECUTOR: Yes?

BERNARD: I'm sorry for you.

PROSECUTOR: *Are* you?

BERNARD: And two: Yes, I am. And two: A paste of baking soda and water left in the pan will scrub it clean effortlessly, overnight. Fuck you. (*He exits.*)

End of Scene Three.

SCENE FOUR

✦ ✦ ✦

The courtroom. Day.

All are present, save the JUDGE, *who enters somewhat bedraggled.*

BAILIFF: All rise.

JUDGE: What time is it?

BAILIFF: Your Honor, it is nine A.M.

JUDGE: At night? (*Pause*)

BAILIFF: Your Honor, no.

JUDGE: All right.

DEFENSE ATTORNEY: Your Honor, thank you for coming in early . . . this may, to your ears, be somewhat more-than-unusual. But, I *believe* that we, in these extraordinary circumstances, have today, an opportunity. You know in ancient times the court was, at once, the seat of justice, and of law, of religion, and of political discourse. A "meeting house," if you will. A forum, in which the community aired, exercised, and so *improved* its commerce, morals, and, in this case, its foreign relations.

JUDGE: . . . where am I . . . ? (*Pause*)

PROSECUTOR: Your Honor . . . (JUDGE *holds up a paper.*)

JUDGE: What is this?

BAILIFF: Your Honor, it is a request for continuance . . .

JUDGE: . . . continuance . . .

DEFENSE ATTORNEY: Your Honor, I think that we possess, today, an opportunity . . .

JUDGE: . . . *what* is this . . . ?

BAILIFF: Your Honor, it's . . .

JUDGE: I mean. It's a piece of paper. Right? (*Pause*)

DEFENSE ATTORNEY: If it please the Court. It is a piece of paper.

JUDGE: Is it made from "wheat"?

PROSECUTOR: Your Honor, I believe, that it is made from wood pulp. If it please the court, you have before you a request for continuance, on the part of the defense, which this office most strenuously opposes. On the following grounds.

DEFENSE ATTORNEY: Your Honor. Here, today, in this city. The representatives of two historically warring powers are convened. My client and I . . .

JUDGE: Might I have a glass of water?

BAILIFF: There's one before Your Honor.

JUDGE: Did I take my pill?

BAILIFF: I believe, Your Honor, yes . . . (JUDGE *takes a pill.*) I believe Your Honor *did* take Your Honor's pill.

JUDGE: Well, now, I'm sure. Now, uh, now, um perhaps we can get on with it. I've got to tell you fellas, after a night of no sleep . . . I'm not feeling too well, and . . .

PROSECUTOR: I opposed, Your Honor, the request, for a continuance . . .

JUDGE: They changed my prescription.

PROSECUTOR: Your Honor—

JUDGE: My first one was putting me to sleep. But I stopped taking it.

PROSECUTOR: Your Honor. I . . .

JUDGE: Gimme a pill. One second. Could you give me a pill?

BAILIFF: Your Honor, the side effect of overdosing . . .

JUDGE: What? Do they make me drowsy?

BAILIFF: Your Honor, *no*. The *others* made you drowsy. The side effects of *this* pill include, uh, oh, (*He reads the label.*) "psychotomimetic" . . . uh . . .

JUDGE: Well, we're just going to have to risk it. *If* justice is to be served. (*He reads.*) What is "Bunny"?

PROSECUTOR: I beg Your Honor's pardon, that is a personal note. (*He goes to retrieve the note.*)

DEFENSE ATTORNEY: Your Honor, if I might address the issue . . .

JUDGE: Why does it want to lick you all over? (*Pause*)

DEFENSE ATTORNEY: Your Honor . . . we have. In our city today. The representatives of Two Great Nations . . .

JUDGE: . . . and something's very wrong here.

DEFENSE ATTORNEY: What, Your Honor?

PROSECUTOR: Indeed it is. The request, for a continuance, leaving aside the lack of simple human concern for Your Honor's health . . .

JUDGE: I mean with this note. (*Pause*) There is something quite wrong with this note. You. You received a note, which I find stuck to my motion. Is that true?

PROSECUTOR: (*Pause*) Yes, Your Honor.

JUDGE: It's signed "Bunny." (*Pause*)

PROSECUTOR: Yes, Your Honor. It is.

JUDGE: *RABBITS CAN'T WRITE.* (*Pause*)

(*A phone rings.* PROSECUTOR *takes out his cell phone.*)

PROSECUTOR: (*To cell phone*) Don't call me here . . .

DEFENSE ATTORNEY: Your Honor, there is a Force For Good, what matter we call it. Some call that force "God."

JUDGE: . . . they can't write.

PROSECUTOR: (*Into phone*) . . . because I'm at work . . .

DEFENSE ATTORNEY: . . . what matter if we picture, in our mind, an ancient man . . . or woman, with a long white beard. Or if we name it but "A Power." We humans are imbued, say "chemically," if you must, with the disposition to *intuit* such a force. If it leads us toward good. Is it not God?

PROSECUTOR: (*Into phone*) I can't talk now . . .

JUDGE: (*To* PROSECUTOR) Would you address yourself to that?

PROSECUTOR: I shall, Your Honor . . . the mention of "God," in a Court of Law . . .

JUDGE: I mean, to the Rabbit. (*Pause*)

PROSECUTOR: The Rabbit, Your Honor, is not a Legal Document.

JUDGE: Then it should not have been found on my desk.

PROSECUTOR: It was, unfortunately, Your Honor, stuck to the motion for continuance.

JUDGE: How?

PROSECUTOR: With the au jus, if you will, of pot roast.

JUDGE: I can't take any more. (*Rising*)

DEFENSE ATTORNEY: Your Honor. If Your Honor, please . . . Sir. The warring representatives of Israel and Palestine are, today in our city. My client and I, we believe, may have constructed . . .

DEFENDANT: *Have* constructed, Your Honor, a method, whereby . . .

PROSECUTOR: (*Into phone*) I said I can't talk now . . .

DEFENSE ATTORNEY: A method, Your Honor, devised by this good man, which, we believe, may bring peace to the Middle East. We crave the court's indulgence, to be given leave to present him and his method to these two world leaders, who, today, are convened, Your Honor . . . In the Name, Your Honor, in the sacred Name of Peace. (*Pause*)

DEFENDANT: We think, Your Honor, that this simple procedure could bring about peace.

PROSECUTOR: What kind of bullshit is this? Your Honor . . . ?

JUDGE: . . . don't worry about me . . . they changed my prescription.

DEFENDANT: "Bullshit"?

JUDGE: The other pills were making me drowsy.

DEFENDANT: . . . bullshit?

DEFENSE ATTORNEY: Your Honor, the comments of the Prosecutor . . .

PROSECUTOR: I am in the midst, I beg your pardon, of some, some, some . . . some familial, some . . .

JUDGE: . . . I didn't know you were married . . .

PROSECUTOR: And you waltz in here, with this bullshit, *bullshit* rhetoric. Taking in vain, the Name of Peace, of . . .

DEFENDANT: I . . .

PROSECUTOR: Spawning, this sick, heretic, Liberal Humanistic Pagan Bullshit, about God and "many forms" . . .

DEFENDANT: *WHO DIED AND LEFT YOU BOSS?*

PROSECUTOR: . . . Your Honor . . . ?

DEFENDANT: "Jesus"?

DEFENSE ATTORNEY: Oh. No.

PROSECUTOR: I beg your pardon?

DEFENDANT: Jesus. A *Jew*. Oy. Are we affronted, that He Died on the Cross. And *we* can't mention: Him. Except every third sentence in your bullshit, hypocritical, Goy day . . .

PROSECUTOR: I object . . .

DEFENDANT: In between raping your children, and, and . . .

PROSECUTOR: Your Honor . . .

DEFENDANT: Bombing abortion clinics, and all.

PROSECUTOR: Your Honor, I must strenuously object to this, vicious, vile . . .

DEFENDANT: You fucking goyim, with "your wives named Marge."

JUDGE: *My* wife is named Marge.

DEFENDANT: Oh, my prophetic soul.

DEFENSE ATTORNEY: Your Honor, what my client intended to say, in referring to "your wife named Marge" . . .

PROSECUTOR: What the hell does that mean, My Prophetic Soul?

JUDGE: . . . did I take my pill?

DEFENDANT: It's Shakespeare.

PROSECUTOR: Oh, bullshit.

JUDGE: Why is he talking about my wife?

DEFENDANT: Aha, and why don't you like Shakespeare . . . ?
    Because he was a Jew.

BAILIFF: He was a Jew?

DEFENDANT: You bet your boots.

PROSECUTOR: But that's preposterous.

DEFENDANT: Is it?

PROSECUTOR: Yes.

JUDGE: Why is it preposterous?

DEFENDANT: Why is it preposterous?

PROSECUTOR: It is preposterous because . . . because . . .

DEFENDANT: I'm waiting.

PROSECUTOR: Because: Shakespeare was not a Jew.

JUDGE: What was he?

PROSECUTOR: What was he?

DEFENDANT: Yeah.

PROSECUTOR: He . . . was a *Christian*.

DEFENDANT: No Christian can write that good.

JUDGE: What do you say to that? (*Pause*) Come on, you want me to do something for you, *you* do something for *me*. (*Pause*)

PROSECUTOR: I . . .

JUDGE: Assuage my ignorance.

PROSECUTOR: I, (*Pause*) The question before this court . . .

BAILIFF: He was a Fag. I know he was a Fag.

JUDGE: . . . he was a Fag . . . ? Shakespeare?

BAILIFF: Yup.

JUDGE: "Shakespeare," who they Teach in Schools?

BAILIFF: Your Honor, yes.

PROSECUTOR: Your Honor . . .

JUDGE: To, to, to, to, to the "little children"?

PROSECUTOR: Your Honor, I must object.

JUDGE: Why, are you a Shakespearean scholar?

PROSECUTOR: No, Your Honor—(*Big pause for effect*) I am a homosexual. (*Pause*)

JUDGE: What is it you guys actually "do"? (*Pause*)

PROSECUTOR: Your Honor . . .

JUDGE: *Seriously* . . . (*Long pause*)

DEFENSE ATTORNEY: Your Honor, the respresentatives of two . . .

JUDGE: And could he not have been a Jew *and* a Fag? (*Pause*) Could he not have been Two Things . . . ?

DEFENSE ATTORNEY: Your Honor, we have, today, an Historic Opportunity.

JUDGE: And how am I to decide?

DEFENSE ATTORNEY: Your Honor?

JUDGE: I mean, 'cause, we can't go back, to, uh, Elizabethan times, and see if, uh, if Shakespeare Plucked his Eyebrows.

DEFENSE ATTORNEY: Your Honor . . .

JUDGE: You know, and if he sometimes "forgot," to wear socks with his penny loafers. So: Someone has Got To Decide. (*Pause*) You see, this is the age-old problem facing Jurisprudence. This, see, *this* is the thing you never think of. "Oh, I'd like to sit up there, and sentence people to Death, and have a reserved parking space," and so on. It never occurs to you that there's a *burden* which comes with it. Nooo. The Burden of Office. That burden is . . . (*Pause*) Uh . . . (*Pause*) It's *uncertainty*. (*Pause*)

DEFENSE ATTORNEY: Your Honor, *Tomorrow*, the Representatives of Two Great Powers . . . convened in our city, will depart, if, *IF*. Your Honor . . .

JUDGE: No *wonder* Solomon cut that baby in half! *You* would, too! You fucken Goody Two-Shoes. "*No! Don't* cut it in half. It's a human *being!*" . . . Oh please.

DEFENSE ATTORNEY: Your Honor.

JUDGE: *Spare* me . . .

PROSECUTOR: Your Honor . . .

JUDGE: . . . for the problem . . . give me another pill . . . it is not what fraction into which you will divide the Child; one half, one quarter . . . it's still *dead*, but:

(*Pause*) See how you're listening to me? I like that. When I'm not at work, I miss it. (*He starts to cry.*) But what are one man's sufferings? In this shithole, we call life. Where where whole *populations* . . .

DEFENSE ATTORNEY: Your Honor . . . ?

JUDGE: . . . have to boil their water. (*Slight pause*) What?

DEFENSE ATTORNEY: Your Honor, if I may, that is the subject, which brings us before the Court.

PROSECUTOR: Your Honor, I should like to respond.

JUDGE: Go ahead.

PROSECUTOR: Your Honor, if I may. We "do," as the court put it, neither more or less than the Heterosexuals. With as much right. Under the Law. To Privacy, to Dignity, to . . .

JUDGE: . . . and then you watch black and white films, right? (*Pause*)

PROSECUTOR: Your Honor . . .

JUDGE: What is it offends you in the Color Process?

DEFENSE ATTORNEY: Your Honor, the representatives of Two Great Peoples.

PROSECUTOR: Your Honor, it is not the color process *per se*; but the decay of storytelling, generally acknowledged as concurrent with, though not occasioned by, the introduction of color.

JUDGE: Is that so.

DEFENSE ATTORNEY: Your Honor, Your Honor?

JUDGE: What?

DEFENSE ATTORNEY: Your Honor, we have an infallible plan to bring Peace to the Middle East.

PROSECUTOR: There are fine, *fine* color films.

BAILIFF: *Drums Along the Mohawk* . . .

JUDGE: I saw that film. It has a lot of Indians.

DEFENSE ATTORNEY: Indeed it does, Your Honor.

JUDGE: And that illustrates my point. That *people* . . . what was I saying . . . ?

PROSECUTOR: Your Honor, I can see the Court is tired, and if I may suggest it . . .

JUDGE: Shakespeare was a *Jew*?

BAILIFF: *And* a Fag . . .

PROSECUTOR: You ought to know . . .

BAILIFF: Excuse me?

PROSECUTOR: Who mentioned *Drums Along the Mohawk* . . . ?

BAILIFF: I saw it on the airplane . . .

PROSECUTOR: Where? To Fire Island . . . ?

ALL: (*Gently*) Ooooh . . . (*Phone rings.*)

BAILIFF: No, if you must know, to Ibiza . . .

PROSECUTOR: (*To phone*) Don't call me here.

DEFENSE ATTORNEY: Your Honor . . .

PROSECUTOR: (*To phone*) I did *not* burn the pan. And I did *not* burn the pot roast. And I am at work.

DEFENSE ATTORNEY: Your Honor . . .

JUDGE: Abraham *Lincoln* was a Jew . . .

BAILIFF: He was . . . ?

JUDGE: Look at his *photographs*.

DEFENSE ATTORNEY: Your Honor, the Leaders of Two Middle Eastern . . .

JUDGE: Don't interrupt me, boyo. Do you know what I can *do*? *I* didn't know what I could do, until they stuck me here . . . what do *I* know . . . ? "Danny: How'd you like to be a Judge?" "Sure. What's it entail . . . ?" Sitting up here, reading *National Geographic*. I get *bored*? "Go to jail." You think I'm kidding . . . ?

DEFENDANT: No.

JUDGE: No, what?

DEFENDANT: No, Your Honor.

JUDGE: I said, "I can send 'em to Jail . . . ?" "You bet your ass." "Mickey," I said, "for *what*?" "Anything, Dan. Anything, or nothing." First time did it feel funny? *Sure*. Like anything. You get used to it. Like sex. You get married. "I can get it anytime." Weeks pass, you *realize*: There have to be *rules*. A pattern, perhaps, give-and-take. Sometimes she's tired . . . the things, what are they called . . . ?

PROSECUTOR: "Precedents"? (*Phone rings.*)

JUDGE: *Vibrators*. They aren't called *precedents*. Huh? Are you *fucking* with me?

PROSECUTOR: (*To phone*) *What?*

DEFENDANT: . . . Your . . .

JUDGE: What would a "precedent" be doing in your bedside table? (*Pause*)

DEFENSE ATTORNEY: Your Honor . . .

JUDGE: *Is* there a limit on my power? Pal? You don't want to know.

PROSECUTOR: Your Honor, I have a family situation . . .

JUDGE: First time I have a mother and her kid. Dad didn't want to pay child support. The mother starts to cry. A more experienced man would have imposed some, some, what are they called . . . ?

BAILIFF: Judicial penalty.

JUDGE: Hey, *you* should be doing this job. On the *guy*. I sent the *kid* to jail.

PROSECUTOR: For *what*?

JUDGE: I don't need a *reason*; all's I need's, this little *hammer* here . . . N'I'm gone use it till the *batteries* run out. (JUDGE *looks around*.) Where is it? All day I'm thinking: What can I do next? I'm *limited*, though, see, by, uh, by . . .

DEFENSE ATTORNEY: . . . by The Law?

JUDGE: Yeah, where's my little hammer? Till I learn about this . . . *What* is it?

BAILIFF: Community service.

JUDGE: Community service. *Now* I'm like: "Uh, find a city park, and cut the grass with your teeth" . . . "tie your clothes into knots, and stuff 'em down the toilet." Uh . . . "shove a *tomato* up your ass," uh . . .

DEFENDANT: . . . how would that benefit the community? (*Pause*)

JUDGE: You're kidding.

DEFENDANT: No. (*Pause*)

JUDGE: While the offender is so-engaged, is he out exposing himself to schoolchildren . . . ?

DEFENDANT: No.

JUDGE: Then shut the fuck up.

PROSECUTOR: Begging the Court's pardon.

JUDGE: Fuck you, you little Suck-Ass. What do you say to that?

PROSECUTOR: Your Honor. (*Hangs up phone*) A pressing, a *pressing* familial need, Your Honor, *forces* me to *ask* Your Honor, if we could return to the pro . . .

JUDGE: And they're called *vibrators*. *I* oughta know.

DEFENSE ATTORNEY: Your Honor. We have a plan to bring Peace to the Middle East.

JUDGE: My God, Man. Why haven't you Spoke Up?

DEFENSE ATTORNEY: We have here a method, arrived at by my client . . .

JUDGE: Do you think I'm Made of Stone?

DEFENSE ATTORNEY: The representatives of Two Great Powers.

JUDGE: Do you think one Little Comment at the nineteenth hole *disqualifies* me from feeling for the Poor Jews?

DEFENSE ATTORNEY: No, Your Honor, no.

JUDGE: The poor persecuted Jews and Arabs?

PROSECUTOR: . . . Your . . .

JUDGE: . . . who slog it out in heat and in *humidity* we civilized, white folk cannot *imagine* . . . ?

PROSECUTOR: . . . Your . . .

JUDGE: *Fuck* that. *Yes.* The White Race is unsuited, yes, to labor in that Equatorial Heat. God, in His mercy, assigned *this* people to *rule* and that to *work.* The Darkies, in the field, bent over, singing, swinging their hips in that rhythmic . . . that . . . that . . .

BAILIFF: Your Honor . . .

JUDGE: You know what, I want to confess . . .

BAILIFF: Your Honor, may I . . .

JUDGE: Gimme my pills.

BAILIFF: Your Honor, may I have those, please . . . ? (BAILIFF *takes the pills.*)

JUDGE: I want to confess.

BAILIFF: Your Honor, the listed side effects for your prescription . . .

JUDGE: Fuck that, into a cocked hat. I want to confess.

BAILIFF: Court is adjourned . . .

JUDGE: Unh *Uh*, Unh *Uh.*

BAILIFF: Your Honor . . .

JUDGE: Everyone else gets to confess. You guilty, guilty scum. "The dog ate my homework." "I had a Twinkie, that's why I shot the Pope." What fucking bullshit. And I am forced, in the name of a "paycheck," to, to feed my "little ones," Lil Mickey, Lil Sue. Susie? What did I do? Susie I, I was *drunk*. That ever happen to you? One night. I swear to God one night. Two nights, at most. Susie? I didn't think that you'd *remember*.

BAILIFF: . . . court is adjourned . . .

(*The* BAILIFF *starts to lead the* JUDGE *away.*)

JUDGE: Do kids remember that far back?

BAILIFF: Your Honor . . .

JUDGE: *Do* they? *I* don't know. I'm asking. Anybody have kids?

PROSECUTOR: I . . .

JUDGE: I just can't take the burden anymore. What am I . . . *Switzerland*? A country with no *feelings* . . . ? You think that I don't have feelings? What do you think, I'm made of Curds and Whey? I'm flesh and blood, like any other man. Look, look, look, if you *cut* me, do I not bleed? Gimme that letter opener.

(*The* BAILIFF *succeeds in hustling the* JUDGE *out of the chamber.*)

BAILIFF: Short recess . . . (*Pause*)

PROSECUTOR: Well. It seems . . .

(*The* JUDGE *comes back into the courtroom, the* BAILIFF *behind him.*)

BAILIFF: All rise.

DEFENSE ATTORNEY: Your Honor, my client and I . . .

JUDGE: Do you know, I once had an affair, with the Only Ugly Girl in Iceland . . . ? (*Pause*) Now, you say how ugly was she . . . ? (*Pause*)

ALL: How ugly was she . . . ?

JUDGE: How ugly do you think she was?

DEFENSE ATTORNEY: Your Honor: (*He reads from his petition.*) "How can the Unitary be Divided? How can the sundered be conjoined . . . ? Through fluid, dynamic stasis . . .

DEFENDANT: . . . brought about . . .

DEFENSE ATTORNEY: . . . through rationalization of the ligatures and, thus, the osteoporotic stem of life.

DEFENDANT: . . . the spine.

DEFENSE ATTORNEY: Thus conducing . . .

DEFENDANT: Yes . . .

DEFENSE ATTORNEY: . . . to peace. Christ's brilliance . . ."

JUDGE: "Jesus" Christ?

DEFENDANT: . . . I thought that we weren't going to put that in . . . ?

DEFENSE ATTORNEY: No, we agreed.

JUDGE: "*Jesus*" Christ . . . ?

DEFENSE ATTORNEY: Well, yes. Yes. Your Honor? We have a petition . . .

DEFENDANT: I thought you were going to take that out . . .

DEFENSE ATTORNEY: If Your Honor would consent, merely, *merely*: to release us, for—(*Checks his watch*)—the next half hour, we, Christian and Jew, have a method . . .

JUDGE: "No no no I will not let you go." Who said that? *Anybody* . . . ?

PROSECUTOR: Pharaoh.

JUDGE: I'm gonna take my clothes off. (*He starts to do so. The* BAILIFF *tries to restrain him.*)

BAILIFF: Your Honor . . .

DEFENSE ATTORNEY: Your Honor:

JUDGE: What . . . ?

DEFENSE ATTORNEY: Christ's brilliance, Christ's brilliance, Your Honor, like that of Moses, like that of the Prophet . . .

JUDGE: The Prophet.

DEFENSE ATTORNEY: Mohammed.

JUDGE: Mohammed. The Prophet of Islam.

DEFENSE ATTORNEY: That's right.

JUDGE: (*Now stripped down to his undershirt*) Whoa, whoa, whoa, then, let's be Very Careful what we say about them. (*Pause*)

DEFENSE ATTORNEY: Their Teachings . . .

JUDGE: . . . hold on: Let's slow it *down*: the the the, the people we're *talking* about.

DEFENSE ATTORNEY: Yes.

JUDGE: With the "things" . . . around their head . . .

DEFENSE ATTORNEY: Yes . . .

JUDGE: Their "teachings" . . .

PROSECUTOR: Ancient, *ancient* religion . . .

DEFENSE ATTORNEY: Consist in a message of Peace. (*Pause*)

JUDGE: I don't think they can object to that, can they?

DEFENSE ATTORNEY: Your Honor, no. (*Pause*)

JUDGE: Those, fine, fine people . . .

DEFENSE ATTORNEY: Um . . .

JUDGE: Because I'd hate to tick them off.

PROSECUTOR: I'm with you *there*, Your Honor.

JUDGE: And I'm not just saying that because they have all the oil . . .

PROSECUTOR: No.

DEFENDANT: No.

DEFENSE ATTORNEY: No.

PROSECUTOR: No indeed.

JUDGE: Or, because they sometimes, uh, uh, uh, uh, they sometimes . . .

DEFENSE ATTORNEY: . . . Everybody needs to "blow off steam" . . .

JUDGE: But because, uh, uh . . . (*Pause*)

PROSECUTOR: Because of their "contributions."

JUDGE: Boy, you've got it there . . .

DEFENDANT: That's for sure.

BAILIFF: I love the integrity of their native textiles. (*Pause*)

(*A murmur of general agreement.*)

DEFENSE ATTORNEY: And the teachings of these wonderful people . . .

JUDGE: Uh huh . . .

DEFENSE ATTORNEY: Consist, as I have said, in a message of Peace.

JUDGE: You're goddamn right they do. But what does it mean, when little children have to go to sleep every night, in garments which are too tight, revealing the various curves of their body to anybody with the least little bit of curiosity?

DEFENSE ATTORNEY: Your Honor . . .

JUDGE: . . . would you address yourself to that?

DEFENSE ATTORNEY: Your Honor, we can bring Peace to the Middle East. (*Pause*)

JUDGE: Is this a "test"?

DEFENSE ATTORNEY: No, Your Honor. It's true.

JUDGE: How you gonna do it?

DEFENSE ATTORNEY: My client believes that the imbalance in their countries, as reflected in their leaders, can be rectified by a readjustment of . . .

JUDGE: You want to bring Peace to the Middle East.

DEFENDANT: Yes, Your Honor.

JUDGE: Whoa. Whoa. That's a big one. And I would *hate* to be the guy who stood in your way. Those two, what, benighted Peoples, warring . . . the Curse of War brought upon them by . . . uh . . . How seldom is it given to us? To bind the wounds—not only of the widow, but the orphan, those little tykes . . . (*Weeps*) May I have a hanky?

DEFENSE ATTORNEY: Your Honor.

JUDGE: No, no, okay! You wanna go lay your plan for Peace, at the feet of those warring powers—

DEFENSE ATTORNEY: No, Your Honor, we want to manipulate their neck.

JUDGE: Sounds good to *me*.

DEFENSE ATTORNEY: Your Honor, then yes, only, if you would release us . . .

JUDGE: By Jove, I *will* then.

DEFENSE ATTORNEY: Bless you, Your . . .

JUDGE: Watch *this*! (*To* BAILIFF) Order a car. I want a police car and escort to take these two gentlemen to present their petition to the Peace Conference. And now: By the power vested in me, yes to exercise compassion, it gives me great pleasure, to, as per my judicial prerogative, and for the purposes of world peace, to release the . . .

BERNARD: (*Enters with a large suitcase. Unable to see, he addresses the air squinting.*) YOU LYING SWINE. I HAVE BEEN WAITING AT *YOUR* MOTHER'S FOR THE LAST FIVE HOURS. THE QUICHE IS COLD, THE CAPRESE SALAD'S HOT, SHE AND I HAVE, AS YOU KNOW, NOTHING IN COMMON SAVE OUR HISTORY OF BABY-

ING *YOU,* YOU DECEITFUL, FORGETFUL,
FAT, SLOVENLY . . .

JUDGE: . . . who is he talking to . . . ?

BERNARD: . . . UNGRATEFUL . . .

JUDGE: . . . 'cause, if he's talking to me, that's contempt.

BERNARD: . . . *OLD* . . .

JUDGE: I'm *sure* of that . . .

BERNARD: WHERE *IS* HE? WHERE *IS* HE?

PROSECUTOR: Put your contacts in.

BERNARD: Where *is* he?

PROSECUTOR: *Put your contacts in.*

BERNARD: I cannot "put my contacts in" as I have been
weeping a river of tears and they will not "go" in.

PROSECUTOR: Bunny . . .

JUDGE: Did you say you wanted to "crick their *neck*"?

BERNARD: And now I'm weeping in front of your friends.
Perhaps you'd introduce me . . .

PROSECUTOR: I . . .

BERNARD: . . . or are you ashamed of me . . . ? You ashamed of me in front of your Straight Friends? "Oh, Honey . . . did you *come* yet . . . ?"

JUDGE: What's wrong with asking that?

BERNARD: . . . if you have to *ask* . . .

JUDGE: I always thought it was *polite* . . .

BERNARD: Of course you did. (*To* PROSECUTOR) And you might ask: What is this? *This* is a *suitcase*. What's in it, you wonder . . .

PROSECUTOR: Bernard . . .

BERNARD: Oooh, our *life* together . . . oh . . .

PROSECUTOR: Bernard . . .

BERNARD: You wouldn't even take my *call* . . .

PROSECUTOR: I'm trying a *case*.

BERNARD: Oh, bullshit.

PROSECUTOR: I'm trying a *case, can't you see that*?

BERNARD: Don't you use that tone with me.

PROSECUTOR: Buns.

BERNARD: Don't you "Buns" me, you . . . you . . . words
fail me . . . *I* don't know. You try to be a *helpmate*.
You try to Care . . . you hope there is a God. Who
sees you . . . who? (*He dissolves in tears. Pause*)

DEFENSE ATTORNEY: Your Honor. There exists, today
only, the, perhaps the last best hope to bring Peace
to the Middle East. My client and I, though of Dif-
ferent Faiths . . .

BERNARD: OH, FUCK *YOU*. HOW CAN YOU HAVE
PEACE IN THE MIDDLE EAST WHEN YOU
CAN'T HAVE PEACE IN YOUR *HOME* . . . ?

JUDGE: . . . you know, you're right . . .

BERNARD: (*Pointing at* PROSECUTOR) Tell *him* that. Tell
him. He's the one that should be on Trial . . .

PROSECUTOR: . . . Bunny . . .

BERNARD: He *abused* me, he was *cruel* to me, and then,
when I went home to *mother*, what was his responsi-
bility?

JUDGE and DEFENDANT and DEFENSE ATTORNEY: To come
after you.

BERNARD: You're goddamn *right* to COME AFTER ME, which is the one, *inviolable* law.

JUDGE: He's right.

BERNARD: In anticipation of which, I made a quiche, a *quiche* offering. When *he* was in the wrong.

JUDGE: Huh.

BERNARD: AND IT'S *HIS* GODDAMN *MOTHER*.

(*All mumble.*)

JUDGE: (*To* PROSECUTOR) That's some fella you've got yourself then . . .

BERNARD: I want to make a complaint: Your Honor . . .

JUDGE: This is the most irregular . . .

BERNARD: I ACCUSE . . . (*Holds up the legal pad he has pulled from his suitcase*)

JUDGE: . . . but-what-the-hell . . .

BERNARD: *I ACCUSE THAT MAN* OF . . . (*He consults his legal pad.*)

PROSECUTOR: Bunny, I'm trying to *work* here . . .

BERNARD: . . . of boorishness. (*Peers at the pad*)

PROSECUTOR: Bun . . .

BERNARD: . . . I'm not done . . . And a lack of sensitivity.

JUDGE: (*To* PROSECUTOR) If this is true, you have a *lot* to answer for . . .

PROSECUTOR: Your Honor . . .

JUDGE: To have the love of a fine young man . . .

BERNARD: Thank you, Your Honor . . .

JUDGE: And to . . . what? *What* did he do . . . ?

BERNARD: He ruined the ROASTING PAN. (*Takes roasting pan from suitcase. Puts it on bench*)

JUDGE: . . . this pan is fine.

BERNARD: He ruined the *roast* . . . I cleaned it with baking soda. He ruined our evening; and he *revealed* to me the essential emptiness, not only of *our* life, but of *my* life . . . (*He cries.*)

JUDGE: . . . come up here . . .

BERNARD: No, NO, I don't deserve affection.

JUDGE: . . . sssshhhhhhh . . .

BERNARD: I deserve *nothing* . . . that's why . . . time after time . . .

JUDGE: Hush . . .

BERNARD: What am I? A hot water bottle . . . a Trick with his name on the lease . . . (*Weeps*)

JUDGE: Sshhh. Nothing's that bad . . .

BERNARD: Time after time . . . Huh. Can I pick 'em . . . Your Honor?

BAILIFF: You mustn't blame yourself.

JUDGE: *Listen* to the man.

BERNARD: Cook, clean, understand when he's too tired to Make Love . . .

JUDGE: Sshhh.

BERNARD: And who is it, takes care of his mother? (*Pause, cries some more*)

DEFENSE ATTORNEY: Wait— . . . excuse me, are they a Bunch of Fags . . . ?

BERNARD: Why, why, why, *why* Can't There Be Peace . . . ?

DEFENSE ATTORNEY: . . . are they *queer*? Is that the punch line . . . ?

(BERNARD *Weeps.*)

JUDGE: There, there, little fella . . .

BERNARD: . . . all I ever wanted was to make a *home* . . . for some *man*.

JUDGE: Sshhh . . .

DEFENSE ATTORNEY: (*Generally*) *These* guys are queer as a v-neck sweater . . .

BERNARD: . . . wash his *clothes* . . . each year, the waistband on his shorts gets bigger. Do *I* complain . . . ?

DEFENSE ATTORNEY: (*To himself*) . . . they're a Bunch of *Fags* . . .

PROSECUTOR: Objection.

(BERNARD *Weeps.*)

JUDGE: I had a dream the other night. Of a clean land, untroubled by pollution. Untroubled by strife. With liberty and with compassion for *all* its citizens. A land administered by people of good faith and self-respect, which stood as an Example To The Nations. Which reached out to them. And stilled their torment with aid: with food, with medicine, with love and understanding.

DEFENSE ATTORNEY: . . . Your Honor . . .

JUDGE: And then this Big Fat Fucking *Dinosaur* came by and *stomped* everybody into moosh. (*Pause*)

DEFENSE ATTORNEY: . . . Your Honor . . .

JUDGE: I think he came from Japan.

DEFENSE ATTORNEY: There exists . . .

JUDGE: I *believe* his size was the result of nuclear testing.

DEFENSE ATTORNEY: The possibility of bringing Peace to the Middle East.

JUDGE: But I don't remember how the dinosaur got there in the first place.

PROSECUTOR: He was a lizard, begging Your Honor's pardon, from the Pet Shop.

JUDGE: . . . what was he doing in my dream?

PROSECUTOR: It wasn't a dream, it was a movie.

DEFENSE ATTORNEY: . . . Your Honor . . .

JUDGE: It was a *movie?*

PROSECUTOR: Yes, Your Honor.

JUDGE: Is it hot in here, or is it just me?

DEFENSE ATTORNEY: Your Honor: As we speak, two great World Leaders, as we speak, are engaged in this historic conference. Have met, in Good Faith, we believe. To attempt to settle the strife in the Middle East. We have devised a plan, which we feel, if it could be represented to them, would bring about that blessed result.

PROSECUTOR: And what *is* this plan?

DEFENSE ATTORNEY: (*To* DEFENDANT) Tell them. (DEFENDANT *mumbles.*) . . . go on . . . (DEFENDANT *mumbles. A pause*) Your Honor, my client believes, and has demonstrated to me, how a simple readjustment of that which very well may prove to be the fifth lumbar vertebra, may, THROUGH A DECREASE IN THE SUBDURAL MFFMFF, RESTORE MENTAL BALANCE TO THE LEADERS AND, through them, to the populace of the Middle East.

PROSECUTOR: Your Honor, the case before this court . . .

JUDGE: I know the case before this court. What do you think I am, Deaf? I'm not deaf. (*To* BAILIFF) I'm not deaf am I, because then I couldn't hear myself. (*To self*) Mooooo . . . Mooo . . . Mooo . . .

BAILIFF: Your Honor, I've taken the liberty of asking a physician . . .

JUDGE: The *question* is: Was Shakespeare a Jew?

PROSECUTOR: Your Honor . . . ?

JUDGE: Or was he a Normal Human Being? (*To* BERNARD) My golly, you smell good.

BERNARD: Thank you, Your Honor.

JUDGE: Call me Danny . . .

BERNARD: Thank you, Danny. You're a Nice Man.

JUDGE: Oh, hush. Because I want to tell you: You bring Peace to the Middle East, and you're gonna look back on it as one of the Proudest Days of Your Life.

DEFENSE ATTORNEY: Your Honor.

JUDGE: Was Shakespeare a Jew? You go first. Whaddaya say?

PROSECUTOR: Your Honor, the introduction of Religion, into a Court of Law . . .

JUDGE: Don't take that tone with me. Jeez. You can't even be civil with your *Boyfriend* . . . (*Pause*) What *did* he do?

BERNARD: He made me burn the pot roast.

JUDGE: YOU *SWINE*. You come *in* here, with your, your highfalutin' tales of Peace and, all the what, the lions will lie down with the lambs. *Bullshit. Bullshit*, is what I say. Pure *Bullshit*.

PROSECUTOR: . . . Your Honor . . .

JUDGE: Because the fucking *lambs* are *already* lying down with the lambs.

PROSECUTOR: Your . . .

JUDGE: At *nighttime*. What are the fucking lambs gonna do? "Yawn yawn, time to turn in, think I'll go bunk with the *lions*"?

BERNARD: No.

JUDGE: You're fucking A. They're *going* to lie down with the lambs. Now . . .

PROSECUTOR: Your Honor . . .

JUDGE: The *lions*, on the other hand: They're never *ever* going to lie down with the lambs. THEY'RE GOING TO EAT THEM.

DEFENSE ATTORNEY: Your Honor, they depart tomorrow. But for the moment, in these fleeting moments, the representatives of two great and warring powers . . .

JUDGE: Do you believe those sheenies and those . . . uh, uh . . .

BAILIFF: . . . fine, upstanding Arabs . . .

ALL: Mmm.

JUDGE: . . . can ever stop their stupid bitching?

PROSECUTOR: He didn't look like a Jew in his pictures . . .

JUDGE: Pictures are deceiving. Did you know that Theodore Roosevelt was a Mulatto?

DEFENSE ATTORNEY: Your Honor, my client . . .

JUDGE: Your client. Yeah, yeah. What did he do? What is it? Insider trading?

DEFENSE ATTORNEY: Your . . .

JUDGE: Child molestation? *We're* all friends here . . .

DEFENSE ATTORNEY: Your Honor, my client has pleaded Not Guilty, to . . .

JUDGE: Well, DUH, *I* get it. *I'm* in on the joke. I understand. All that he's got to do. Okay, *off* the record, just for the, the, the, you concur . . .

PROSECUTOR: Your Honor, make him say "I'm sorry."

JUDGE: You bet. Come on now.

BERNARD: Would somebody help me find my contact?

JUDGE: Whatever the fellow did, you have him come up here n'say "I'm sorry"—then we'll save the Middle East. (*Pause*)

(DEFENDANT *and* DEFENSE ATTORNEY *confer.*)

DEFENSE ATTORNEY: Your Honor, my client has asked me to forward to this Honorable Court his statement, which consists in but those two, blest, blessed words: I'M SORRY.

PROSECUTOR: Make him *say* it.

JUDGE: Say it, pal.

(*All murmur.* DEFENDANT *comes forward.*)

BERNARD: I think that he should say it.

DEFENDANT: I'm sorry.

JUDGE: I CAN'T HEAR YOU.

DEFENSE ATTORNEY: Speak up, please.

DEFENDANT: I'm sorry.

JUDGE: That's all it takes. And now:

BERNARD: I know that voice . . . I KNOW THAT VOICE . . . GEORGE BERNSTEIN? *IS THAT YOU?* IS THAT YOU, YOU SONOFABITCH?

DEFENDANT: I, I . . .

BERNARD: HOW DARE YOU COME IN HERE AND SHOW YOUR FACE?

DEFENSE ATTORNEY: Who is George Bernstein?

BERNARD: After you hung me out to dry in Hawaii? You sonofabitch.

PROSECUTOR: Who is George Bernstein?

BERNARD: And you gave me a False NAME?

DEFENDANT: Bunny. Buns . . .

BERNARD: Don't you "Buns" me. I sat in that hotel room Three Days, waiting for you to come back from the Ice Dispenser.

DEFENDANT: Bunny. My wife.

JUDGE: Bunny . . . ?

BERNARD: Eating macadamia nuts. Do you have any *notion* the amount of carbohydrates I consumed?

DEFENDANT: Bunny, I wanted to stay, my wife.

BERNARD: "Oh Bunny, let me Take you to Hawaii . . ."

PROSECUTOR: . . . take you to Hawaii . . .

JUDGE: "Bunny." I *know* that name . . .

PROSECUTOR: YOU LITTLE WHORE. HE TOOK YOU TO HAWAII? WHEN?

BERNARD: Last November.

DEFENDANT: Bunny, my wife called, she . . .

PROSECUTOR: You told me you were going to Atlantic City with My Mother.

BERNARD: I lied, I lied, all right? D'that ever happen to you?

DEFENSE ATTORNEY: Your Honor . . .

PROSECUTOR: Where did you meet him?

BERNARD: Is it important?

PROSECUTOR: I want to know.

BERNARD: The small leather-goods counter at Saks.

DEFENSE ATTORNEY: Your Honor . . .

BERNARD: He was buying an agenda.

DEFENSE ATTORNEY: Your Honor, for the remainder of today . . .

PROSECUTOR: Your Honor, I *have* that agenda . . .

DEFENSE ATTORNEY: Scant moments, during which we may bring peace to the Middle . . .

PROSECUTOR: Your Honor, I have that agenda in evidence, which . . . Wait wait wait wait *wait* MY MOTHER HELPED YOU CHEAT ON ME . . . ?

(DOCTOR *enters*.)

DOCTOR: I'm sorry I'm late.

JUDGE: And who is this, now?

DOCTOR: (*To* BAILIFF) Show me the bottle. How many pills did he take?

BAILIFF: Your Honor, I've taken the liberty of contacting a physician . . .

DOCTOR: I'm sorry that I'm late, Your Honor. I was delayed by the extraordinary security precautions attendant upon the end of the Middle East Peace Conference.

PROSECUTOR: You and my mother . . . *Bunny* . . . ?

JUDGE: "Bunny." His Name was Stuck to the Note on the Motion.

DOCTOR: Give me your arm, please . . .

JUDGE: With the Au Jus of a Pot Roast . . .

DOCTOR: Mm, hmm. Give me your arm, please. (DOCTOR *takes hypodermic from his bag.*)

JUDGE: This is no time to get high.

BERNARD: My name . . . ?

JUDGE: On the note it said, it said . . . (*Handing up the note*) Here. "I want to Lick You All Over. Bunny."

DOCTOR: Give me your arm, please.

JUDGE: I can't right now, I'm busy—we're bringing peace to the Mid-East.

DOCTOR: How are you going to do that?

JUDGE: We're going to crick their necks.

DEFENDANT: That is a simplified, but an essentially correct . . .

DOCTOR: This man is in the throes of a drug-induced psychotomimetic fugue.

JUDGE: And what the fuck's it *to* you?

DOCTOR: (*To* BAILIFF) Subdue him, please.

DEFENDANT: I don't believe he needs a shot . . .

DOCTOR: Excuse me?

DEFENDANT: He does not require an injection.

DOCTOR: And now you speak in what capacity?

DEFENDANT: I speak as a Chiropractor.

DOCTOR: No, seriously . . .

DEFENDANT: Are you ignorant of the fact, a heightened state of mental aggravation can be lessened, without drugs, as has been known for fifteen million years, by a simple reversal of the lumbar subluxation?

DOCTOR: Blow me.

DEFENDANT: EXCUSE MEEEE . . . ?

DOCTOR: Subdue the patient, please . . .

DEFENDANT: "BLOW ME"???

DOCTOR: Oh, is it mad because it didn't get into medical school . . . ? Subdue the patient please.

DEFENDANT: Excuse me . . . ? Excuse me . . . ? Excuse me . . . ?

(*The* DEFENDANT *crawls up over the bench and begins strangling the* DOCTOR.)

DEFENDANT: Well, how about that? How about that, huh? Does that feel good . . . ?

DOCTOR: Ow. Ow ow ow . . . (*Et cetera*)

DEFENDANT: How about that, huh? Is that as much fun as pimping for the insurance companies?

DOCTOR: Help . . .

DEFENDANT: Huh? Huh? And selling your soul for an ash-tray?

DOCTOR: Help . . .

DEFENDANT: With some drug company's name on it . . . ?

JUDGE: Where's my gavel . . . ?

DOCTOR: Help, help . . .

JUDGE: . . . where's my fucking gavel . . . ?

DEFENDANT: Didn't teach you *this* in medical school, *did* they? (*Kicks* DOCTOR)

DOCTOR: Help . . .

DEFENDANT: . . . when they gave you that stupid white coat . . . (*Pause*)

BERNARD: Wait a ssss . . . (*Appeals to* JUDGE) Your Honor . . . ?

JUDGE: They took my fucking gavel . . .

DEFENDANT: Cure *cancer* you arrogant *fuck*!

BERNARD: (*Bangs on bench with roasting pan*) Wait a second, wait a second, wait a second! (*Pause*)

JUDGE: What?

BERNARD: The note said "I want to lick you all over. Bunny"?

JUDGE: Yes.

(BERNARD *begins weeping.*)

JUDGE: What?

BERNARD: That is the note . . . that is the note I wrote him, after our First Date. (*To* PROSECUTOR) You *kept* it . . . ?

PROSECUTOR: I've carried it. All this time. In my pocket.

BERNARD: No . . .

PROSECUTOR: (*Starting to cry*) Yes . . .

BERNARD: All this *time*?

PROSECUTOR: That's right.

BERNARD: Oh, I've been SO wrong . . .

PROSECUTOR: Bunny . . .

BERNARD: Can you *forgive* me . . . ?

PROSECUTOR: Bunny, in many ways, it's I, who should beg *your* forgiveness . . .

BERNARD: No, no . . .

PROSECUTOR: If I'd been more *attentive* . . .

BERNARD: No, no, you have your work. I *see* that, now.

PROSECUTOR: But, Bunny. But, but I lost a sense of *balance*.

BERNARD: No, no, no, no, no . . .

PROSECUTOR: Which is essential for any ongoing relationship.

(*He weeps. They embrace.*)

JUDGE: You see? This, *this* is what I live for. This is my dream. This is the dream of a Young Jurist. Not the "bribes," yes, yes, we "take" them, but what do we live for? The, the, uh, uh . . .

PROSECUTOR: I want to wipe the slate clean, Bunny, and begin again.

BERNARD: . . . shhh . . .

PROSECUTOR: But I *can't* with this on my soul.

BERNARD: Tell me, and be forgiven. (PROSECUTOR *whispers to* BERNARD.) I *knew.*

PROSECUTOR: What?

BERNARD: I knew *ALL THE TIME* . . .

BAILIFF: . . . *What? (Pause)*

PROSECUTOR: Oh Bunny, how could I deserve you, you . . . (*They weep.*)

DOCTOR: *I* want to confess . . . *I* want to confess . . .

PROSECUTOR: Oh, Bunny . . .

DOCTOR: Once, with a female patient . . .

DEFENDANT: *I* want to confess . . . I'm *guilty* . . . *guilty* do you hear . . . ? Your Honor, I'm guilty as charged.

BERNARD: What is he accused of? (*Pause*)

DEFENDANT: I attacked a chiropodist. (*All murmur.*) And . . . (*Pause*)

PROSECUTOR: Get it off your chest.

DEFENDANT: And I had sex with a goose. (*He weeps.*)

DEFENSE ATTORNEY: I cheated on my income tax . . .

PROSECUTOR: I never took the Bar exam . . .

JUDGE: *I'm Jewish.* (*Pause*)

DOCTOR: This man's in *shock* . . .

JUDGE: I'm Jewish. My father told me. He confessed.

PROSECUTOR: . . . oh, Your Honor . . .

JUDGE: He came over from Poland. He told everybody he was Welsh. He was a *Jew* . . . my father was a Jew . . . I'm a Jew . . . I'm a sheeny . . . (*Weeps*)

DEFENDANT: You're not a Jew unless your mother was a Jew.

JUDGE: What?

DEFENDANT: You're not a Jew unless your mother was a Jew.

JUDGE: I'm *not* a Jew . . . ?

DEFENDANT: No.

JUDGE: (*Pause*) Thank God. Thank you, God. You do exist. There is a God . . .

DOCTOR: Hold him, while I administer the hypodermic.

JUDGE: There is a God. It's all true. People? People? God *exists.* (*To* BAILIFF) Do you hear? God exists!!! (*He goes to embrace the* BAILIFF.)

DOCTOR: (*Administering the hypodermic*) The antidote should take effect immediately.

JUDGE: God exists. How could we *e'er* repay his Endless Mercies?

DEFENSE ATTORNEY: Your Honor, we could bring peace to the Middle East.

BAILIFF: Your Honor, the car is waiting. I have called ahead, the car is waiting to transport us to the Peace Conference.

(*All start toward the door, save the* JUDGE. *They look back and see the* JUDGE *still seated.*)

BAILIFF: Wait, he has to say, "Court is Adjourned . . ."

JUDGE: Yeah, that's right, I have to, um . . . (*Phone rings.*)

(*All look around to find the culprit guilty of leaving on the ringer.* BERNARD *takes the phone from his pocket.*)

BERNARD: Hello . . . ?

DEFENDANT: If Your Honor will but say, "Court is Adjourned . . ."

BERNARD: (*Apologizing to court, as he opens his phone*) I'm sorry . . . (*To* PROSECUTOR) It's your mother.

PROSECUTOR: I have nothing to say to her.

BERNARD: She wants to know if you're watching the Peace Conference on TV.

PROSECUTOR: Tell her I can't talk now. I'm *working*.

BERNARD: Mom? Mom? He's working . . .

DEFENSE ATTORNEY: If Your Honor will but say, "Court is Adjourned . . ."

BERNARD: (*Reiterating the question of the* PROSECUTOR's *mother*) . . . "Did you hear what the one fellow called the other fellow at the Peace Conference? . . ." . . . *What?* He called the other guy *what* . . . ? ON TV . . . ?

DEFENDANT: What, what did he say?

BERNARD: Can I repeat it in a Court of Law . . . ? He *said* . . .

(*Sound of sirens. All listen.*)

JUDGE: Would somebody turn off the kettle . . . ?

BAILIFF: Your Honor, that is the sound of sirens.

DEFENSE ATTORNEY: The leaders have quitted the Peace Conference. They have departed in wrath.

DEFENDANT: Too late, too late . . . why, Lord, oh why are we doomed to endless strife?

DEFENSE ATTORNEY: Well, everything was going fine till you killed Christ.

(*General approval.* DEFENDANT *gets incensed and attacks the* DEFENSE ATTORNEY.)

JUDGE: Hey, in all fairness, he's right. But that's a question for another day. (JUDGE *raises gavel.*) Case dism—

BAILIFF: One moment. (*Puts his arm around* JUDGE) *Yes,* we may have spent our vacation on Ibiza, but we were on the *straight* part of the island.

ALL: Oh, *please* . . .

JUDGE: (*He looks to* BAILIFF, *who nods. Then the* JUDGE *brings down the gavel.*) This court is adjourned.

END.